My Own
Four Walls

My Own Four Walls

A Philadelphia Newspaper Columnist as Homesteader Between the Wars

DON ROSE

Edited by NEIL GENZLINGER

McFarland & Company, Inc., Publishers
Jefferson, North Carolina

Frontispiece: Don Rose (photograph by Michael Pitcairn).

LIBRARY OF CONGRESS CATALOGUING-IN-PUBLICATION DATA

Names: Rose, Donald Frank, 1890–1964, author. | Genzlinger, Neil, 1954– editor.
Title: My own four walls : a Philadelphia newspaper columnist as homesteader between the wars / Don Rose ; edited by Neil Genzlinger.
Description: Jefferson, North Carolina : McFarland & Company, Inc., Publishers, 2018 | Includes index.
Identifiers: LCCN 2018041816 | ISBN 9781476675930 (softcover : acid free paper) ∞
Subjects: LCSH: Rose, Donald Frank, 1890–1964—Homes and haunts. | Country life—Pennsylvania—Bryn Athyn—Anecdotes. | Farmhouses—Conservation and restoration—Anecdotes. | Dwellings—Maintenance and repair—Anecdotes. | British Americans—Pennsylvania—Biography. | Journalists—Pennsylvania—Biography. | Montgomery County (Pa.)—History, Local. | Bryn Athyn (Pa.)—Biography.
Classification: LCC F159.B79 R67 2018 | DDC 974.8/12—dc23
LC record available at https://lccn.loc.gov/2018041816

BRITISH LIBRARY CATALOGUING DATA ARE AVAILABLE

ISBN (print) 978-1-4766-7593-0
ISBN (ebook) 978-1-4766-3457-9

© 2018 Neil Genzlinger. All rights reserved

No part of this book may be reproduced or transmitted in any form or by any means, electronic or mechanical, including photocopying or recording, or by any information storage and retrieval system, without permission in writing from the publisher.

Front cover artwork by Leon Rose

Printed in the United States of America

McFarland & Company, Inc., Publishers
  Box 611, Jefferson, North Carolina 28640
  www.mcfarlandpub.com

Acknowledgments

Republishing an existing book requires a surprising amount of work, considering that the hard part—the actual writing of the book—has already been done. But being a descendant of Don Rose means that there were plenty of willing hands to help with typing the manuscript, proofreading it, compiling the artwork and other chores. Thanks to those who pitched in, including, from the first generation (that is, Don's children), Frank Rose, Sylvia Cooper and my mother, Muriel Genzlinger.

Other relatives who volunteered their time and effort include Bill Grubb, Judy Stewart, Dale Morris, Chara Daum, Scott Cooper, Daniel Clark, Michelle Rose and probably others I'm forgetting. Also, thanks to editor Dylan Lightfoot at McFarland for shepherding the project, and Lauren Rose Lightfoot for coming up with the idea in the first place.

Neil Genzlinger, fall 2018

Table of Contents

Acknowledgments   v
Preface by Neil Genzlinger   1
My Own Four Walls by Don Rose   7

    I. Of the Landed Gentry   9
   II. Where's the Fire?   15
  III. O Rare Ben Yerkes!   22
  IV. In the Pennypack Valley   29
    V. On Armistice Day, 1918   36
  VI. Be the Same More or Less   42
 VII. Stretching a Shoestring   49
VIII. My House Is Haunted   57
  IX. Hands Are for Handicrafts   64
    X. Curing the Smoking Habit   71
  XI. Cobwebs on the Classics   78
 XII. What Am I Bid?   85
XIII. Why Wives Leave Home   92
XIV. Handy Man Around the House   99
 XV. Bricks Are So Plentiful   107
XVI. Are You a Mason?   115
XVII. Laid on with a Trowel   123

Table of Contents

XVIII.	A Garden of Good Intentions	129
XIX.	The Care and Feeding of Carrots	137
XX.	The Gentleman Farmer	144
XXI.	Confessions of a Fundamentalist	151
XXII.	I Shall Miss My Debts	159
XXIII.	Est Mihi Rus Minimum	168
Index		175

Preface by Neil Genzlinger

As I write this, it is just a few months until the 100th anniversary of the moment when my maternal grandparents, Don and Marjorie Rose, took title to an old farmhouse and about an acre of land in Bryn Athyn, Pa., where they would proceed to raise a very large family. That minor event in the history of real estate but major event in the history of our family occurred on August 16, 1918, when World War I was in its final months and modern conveniences like electric refrigerators were still in the future.

Almost a quarter-century later, Don Rose, by then a well-known Philadelphia newspaper columnist, would write the story of that house in a book he called *My Own Four Walls*—this book. It was originally published in 1941 by Doubleday, Doran & Company, generating a smattering of notices and a smattering of sales, mostly in greater Philadelphia.

Why republish it now? Partly as a window onto the past. Partly for insights it contains that still have value today. And partly for the glimpse into the formative years of a man who, by the time he died in 1964, was a Philadelphia institution and a journalist of national stature.

My Own Four Walls is, in a sense, a book about finding one's place, which makes sense, because before he was a newsman or a husband and father, Don Rose was an immigrant. He was born on June 29, 1890, in the village of Street, in southern England. His parents, Frank Hodson Rose and Mary Searle Rose, were people of modest means but well read; in letters to their son after he came to America, they debated the issues of the day intelligently and at length, the way letter-writers did before email trivialized the art of correspondence. They gave him two younger brothers, three younger sisters and an upbringing in the theology of Emanuel

Preface by Neil Genzlinger

Swedenborg, an 18th-century scientist, scholar and theologian whose claim to a divinely inspired interpretation of the Bible was the basis of a small but influential church.

Don went to work as a clerk in a brewery at 14, but his parents must have known he possessed an intellectual curiosity that needed only to be developed. When a scholarship became available to the Academy of the New Church, a Swedenborgian school outside Philadelphia, they sent him. He arrived at Ellis Island in the fall of 1908, having made the trans-Atlantic passage alone at age 18, part of the great immigration wave that brought millions of people to the United States.

The idea was for him to complete his interrupted high school education and then be trained for the ministry; his father had long harbored a wish of becoming a minister himself. Don got most of the way through theology school before abandoning those efforts for, as he would later write, the good of the church. Instead he ended up teaching at the Academy—English, Latin, Hebrew. In 1914, just before his 24th birthday, he married Marjorie Wells, whom he had been courting since they were in high school together. The next year their first child, Tryn, arrived. By 1918 they had three children and a need for more space than their rented apartment provided. Which brings us to the purchase of the house that is the subject of this book.

Don and Marjorie would eventually have 12 children. (My mother, Muriel, the fourth-oldest, was the first to be born in the house, in 1920.) Don might easily have become a career educator, retiring after a lengthy Academy tenure that would have included teaching some of his own kids. Instead, in 1925, with seven of the 12 offspring now born, things took what must have been a catastrophic turn: He was laid off.

He never wrote much about why; the story in the family was always that the tiny school had to pare three positions down to two and chose him to get the ax on the theory that he was best equipped to survive in the outside world. If so, that would eventually prove true, but first came a difficult stretch of supporting himself with odd jobs while he fashioned a new career. He determined straight away that he wanted to make his living with a pen, but how to go about it?

"I had a suspicion that I could write, if I tried," he recalled later. He had even made occasional efforts to do so, he said. "But in my inner and

Preface by Neil Genzlinger

critical consciousness," he said, "I was quite aware that I was getting nowhere, either in accomplishment or capacity. So I made myself a whip in the form of a monthly magazine."

He called it *Stuff and Nonsense—A Magazine of No Importance*. The term "magazine" was a bit generous; it was more like what would be called a newsletter today. The first issue, in August 1925, consisted of four notebook-size pages and had a staff box that looked like this:

Editor
Donald F. Rose
Assistant Editor
Donald F. Rose
Advertising Manager
Donald F. Rose
Address all communications to
Donald F. Rose

The venture had a very practical motivation: Don used the magazine to advertise his other business ventures. Those included, at various times, selling and servicing oil burners, peddling Universal and Hotpoint appliances and representing Kodak film and projectors. He also offered his services as a writer, and the rental of the Come Again Cabin, an old chicken coop on his property that he had converted into an apartment.

Subscriptions to *Stuff and Nonsense* were $1 a year, and by the end of the first year, in July 1926, he had 300 subscribers. What paid off in the end, though, was his shamelessness about distributing freebies: He sent copies of the sheet to anyone he thought might advance his fledgling writing career. Editors and writers of all sorts received it, and some actually read it. One who did was Jay E. House, a columnist for the *Philadelphia Public Ledger*, the second-largest of the city's 11 daily newspapers, with a circulation of about 340,000. In November 1925 he sent Don a complimentary letter. "It is light, frolicsome writing, well done," he told him. "And God knows, we need more of that sort of thing."

Jay House would become Don's friend and mentor, a connection that would shortly pay off. Meanwhile, *Stuff and Nonsense* continued to gather momentum. An essay in the February 1927 issue made a particular impact. It was called "Menckenism" and was more serious than most of the

Preface by Neil Genzlinger

magazine's offerings, criticizing H.L. Mencken, one of the country's most influential writers, for satirizing easy targets without articulating a positive vision. The piece was cited by numerous other publications, including the *New York Times*.

In the September 1927 issue, Don gave *Stuff and Nonsense* readers some news.

"The editor confesses that he is now responsible for a weekly column under the title of 'Stuff and Nonsense' on the editorial page of the Sunday Public Ledger of Philadelphia," he wrote. "Just how long this thing is going to last is something we can't tell you, but you will perhaps forgive us for telling you that we have at least started it."

As it turned out, "this thing" would last for more than 35 years. Don's first newspaper column appeared on September 25, 1927. The job, surely secured with the help of Jay House, also included writing unsigned editorials for the paper and, beginning in 1929, writing a weekly piece on children's books in the book section. In February 1932 his weekly column became a daily column. one in which—to quote the paper's advertising—he addressed "the familiar absurdities of average existence, the lights and shadows of the domestic comedy, the fads and follies of American life and custom."

That often meant writing about his family, which had rounded out at an even dozen children with the birth of Donald Leslie Rose in 1931. It is young Donald who is credited in family lore with saying, after yet again appearing in the column, "Why doesn't he just beat us, like other fathers?"

Don wrote of many other things as well, with a light and breezy style that for readers must have been a refreshing escape from the woes of the Depression. He built up a significant fan base, which was a good thing, because the *Evening Ledger* was in poor financial condition. When it folded in early 1942, Don and his column were snapped up by the *Philadelphia Evening Bulletin*, which was well on its way to becoming the largest evening newspaper in the country—its circulation would soon top 761,000. If Don Rose was well known before, at the *Bulletin* he became a journalistic star, in the Philadelphia market and beyond.

The column continued to be lighthearted for the most part, although Don's more somber pieces—about a son going off to war, for instance, or the death of his friend, the actor Leslie Howard—were among his finest.

Preface by Neil Genzlinger

The best work of his career may have come when the paper let him join a War Department tour of some of the bombed-out parts of Europe in July 1945. The idea was to bring outside observers into the war zones of Germany and other countries before the areas could be cleaned up, sometimes literally while bodies remained unburied, to see and record the effects of modern aerial bombardment. Don found lots of horror and glimmers of hope.

"In Hamburg the ruin of buildings is indescribable and inconceivable," he wrote. "But in hundreds of holes beneath the rubble people are living, and have lived there a long time. They live in no better quarters by thousands in Berlin; they eat bad bread and potatoes and drink contaminated water. Under such circumstances they should have died long ago, but life is tough. It is a good thing for the better hopes and purposes of humanity that it is."

Don lost much of his eyesight when he had a stroke in 1963, but he was still writing his "Stuff and Nonsense" column for the *Bulletin* right up until his death on February 7, 1964.

"Day after day, through the years, he provided a pleasant few minutes for thousands," the *Bulletin* wrote the next day in tribute. "But whimsy alone could never have won and held the following that Don Rose possessed among the readers of the old Evening Ledger and, for two decades, the Bulletin. Peeping through the whimsy there was always evidence of a truth that Don Rose, most diffident of men, would never admit: that he was a profoundly learned man with a knowledge of many ancient languages—Greek, Latin, Hebrew and Egyptian hieroglyphics; a man who knew every line of Shakespeare and most of the other classics; a deeply religious man, with a philosophy lightened by unfailing humor and kindness."

A reader named Max Schachter was one of many who wrote to the paper.

"Once I made a Bermuda crossing on the same ship with him, but I was too much in awe to say what I am writing," he wrote. "The subsequent articles that appeared in The Bulletin made the trip seem great and grand and humorous, when actually nothing happened."

Which brings us to *My Own Four Walls*, the book Don published in 1941 and is reproduced here as he wrote it, antiquated spellings and British

Preface by Neil Genzlinger

punctuations (no period in "Mr"!) intact. It is, at first glance, a book in which nothing happens, or at least nothing of great consequence. A couple buys an old house and fixes it up—end of story.

But the telling is worth savoring: droll and affectionate and insightful. So too is the history here. "My Own Four Walls" reminds us that, not very long ago, automobiles were a rarity, electrical appliances were a novelty, and people rebuilt and reused anything they could.

Most of all, though, this book is about one man's efforts to root himself in a particular place, on a particular patch of land. For many in our age of condominium complexes and McMansions, that is a lost art. Don Rose did a deep dive into his chosen location, trying to find out who had lived there before, who had built the structures, what their lives had been like. And he then detailed his own habitation, his home-improvement efforts, his gardening and path-laying and mortgage-retiring. This is a book by a man who knew that a home can be more than just a place to live; it can be your personal chapter in the ongoing story of life.

Don would no doubt be pleased to know that, a century after he bought it, the old farmhouse and its outbuildings, though now squeezed on a crowded suburban street, are still home to some of his descendants. "When you buy a farmhouse with a century of history under its roof," he writes in these pages, "you may expect it to be built well enough to stand a century more." And counting.

My Own Four Walls
by Don Rose

Illustrated by Leon Rose

I

Of the Landed Gentry

A while ago arrived a curious communication in my morning mail. The letter, dated from England, offered me honorable mention in a new edition of a book about the American "landed gentry," professing to include the histories of "5000 distinguished American families of British ancestry."

No visible strings were attached to the offer, except the suggestion that I could secure a copy of the book at the "specially reduced review price of $20." Nor did the letter go into sordid details in identifying me as a member of the landed gentry.

I admit the British ancestry. My land is a fraction over a single acre, approximately half paid for. It hardly seems enough for a member of the landed gentry. I have owned and lived on it for only about twenty-three years, and most of the family has happened since I bought it. The family is large but not notably distinguished, and the British ancestry is only a single generation away.

So I laid the letter aside in the living-room wastebasket. Its implied definition of the landed gentry, evidently, was that they might possibly be landed for $20.

This Who's Who of the landed gentry, by its own confession, traces some of its distinguished American families back to the eighth and ninth centuries of English history. This is not necessarily difficult, for almost everybody has ancestors. It is also alleged on scientific authority that everybody of British descent is related to everybody else by the time the family tree is trimmed back to the Norman Conquest.

But some people like to pick and choose their ancestors. This may account for another letter making a really remarkable offer. For a nominal

My Own Four Walls

fee somebody would run our family tree into the ground, noting on the way all important branches, grafts and suckers. A coat of arms, with or without two pairs of trousers, would be provided for a slight additional charge.

Nothing came of it. In the first place, my wife is a thoroughly American girl, claiming connections with the Mayflower cargo, and not much interested in British ancestors. In any case, a wife's interest in her husband's relatives decreases inversely as the square of the distance.

In the second place, I already owned an impressive and slightly notorious ancestor, the late and unlamented Laurence, Earl of Ferrers, who lived about the middle of the eighteenth century. He lived rather luridly and died suddenly. In fact, he was hanged. His manservant blundered in laying out a dress shirt or something, and there was nothing to do about it but shoot him, for which Laurence, Fourth Earl of Ferrers, was tried by his peers and hanged at Tyburn on May 5, 1760.

Since he was an earl, though an excitable one, his own horses drew his carriage to the execution and he met his end by a noose in a silken rope instead of the customary hemp. This must have been a comfort to his last moments and is duly appreciated by his surviving relatives.

For thirty years I had claimed the earl as a relative, though not a close acquaintance, and referred to him as my favorite ancestor. It spoiled the story somewhat when I looked him up more carefully in Burke's Peerage and discovered that he died a bachelor.

So now we are satisfied with a merely collateral connection, which may be sufficient to entitle me to a coat of arms.

The earl's own coat is bloodstained, and I have designed myself a better. Its crest is a rose in a bottle of ink. Its shield is quartered and shows a safety pin *rampant*, a checkbook *dormant*, the sheriff *regardant* and the stork *indignant*. The whole works is supported by a second-hand typewriter and charge accounts at four Philadelphia department stores.

Long before I had the slightest thought of becoming landed gentry in Montgomery County, Pennsylvania, I was born in a little town named Street, in Somersetshire, England. It was a good place to be born an Englishman. Glastonbury Tor, three miles from my birthplace on Wilfred Terrace, looks down on the scene of thirty centuries of English history. The Glastonbury bowl, a nice piece of work in hammered bronze, was made

I. Of the Landed Gentry

by the Britons of 3000 years ago and was found in the peat moors a few miles from my first home. Down there, too, are remains of the villages of the Sea Moor Settlers from which Somerset got its name.

Glastonbury stands on Avalon Hill, once an island, where King Arthur sailed to be healed of his grievous wounds.

> *To the island-valley of Avilion,*
> *Where falls not hail, or rain, or any snow,*
> *Nor ever wind blows loudly; but it lies*
> *Deep-meadowed, happy, fair with orchard lawns*
> *And bowery hollows crown'd with summer sea.*

On Avalon Hill, too, was built the great Abbey of Glastonbury on the site of Christianity's earliest settlement in western Britain. A sad ruin now, and its fragments are found in house walls, barns and pigsties for miles around. Here rumor has it that the Holy Grail of Arthurian legend is buried, but more likely it is the treasure of Glastonbury which Henry the Eighth could never find. Nor can anybody else, though many have hunted for it.

From the Tor you may also look down on Athelney, where King Alfred meditated gloomily about the Danish campaign and may have burned the cakes. Here was found the Alfred jewel, now in the Ashmolean Museum at Oxford, a trinket of soft gold with the inscription "Alfred Had Me Made." And from the same high hill you may look toward Sedgemoor, until lately the last place where a battle was fought on English soil.

Can you suggest a better place for a Britisher to be born? Better still, to my earliest understanding, was the fact that Grandfather was a cobbler and could tell great tales of Baron Munchausen. "Is it true, Grampa?" I often asked him.

"I read it in a book, sonny," was his answer. Many things, even now, are made true by being written in a book.

It was also a good place to be born because Uncle George Hurford kept pigs there, and Uncle Pat Searle was wise in respect to mushrooms and blackberries, and a creaking windmill stood atop Ivythorn Hill and still did the last time I was there. And there were quarries round about where a small boy might chip fossils from the limestone, and the caves of Cheddar and Wookey Hole not far away.

It was, indeed, a good place to be born. But we left there when I was

My Own Four Walls

seven and lived in London and later in many parts of southeastern England. And it was from the village of Cheam, in Surrey, that I went to work at the age of fourteen and was clerk in an ancient brewery for four years. The beginning salary was $1.50 a week, and by assiduous devotion to duty it increased to $4.00 by the year 1908.

That was when it was decided I should go to America.

The reason was a scholarship available in a sectarian school not far from Philadelphia. The idea was that I should be educated for the ministry, an ambition finally abandoned for the good of the church. But it was sufficient, in 1908, to set me aboard the old St Paul, bound for the United States and whatever else might come of it.

Sometime during the World War of 1914–18 the St Paul ignominiously turned upside down at dockside in New York Harbor. I could have predicted, in 1908, that eventually she would. The St Paul was a stout ship, fast for those days, but is still remembered as one of the most tub-bottomed vessels ever to sail the Atlantic. She did not plow the waves—she rolled over them. The effect on steerage passengers was quickly catastrophic.

Sea travelers of today must take my word for it that it is possible to be abysmally and suicidally seasick for four days. They wouldn't know. They wouldn't know of the six smells that once inhabited the steerage quarters of a deep-sea liner—the fragrances of paint, plumbing, disinfectant, cooking, unwashed humanity and hot engine oil. So six minutes after leaving Southampton I was seasick, recovered briefly while the boat stopped at Cherbourg and was sick again as soon as we passed the breakwater. That was in October, a rough month on anybody's ocean and supremely so on the Atlantic in 1908.

I came out of it suddenly, as seasick sufferers do, when we were half-seas over. And discovered that the loneliest and drabbest place on land or sea, in those days, was the crowded steerage of an ocean liner. Third-class quarters of modern ships are sybaritic palaces in comparison. There was literally nothing to do. Deck privileges were confined to watching the sweated and sooted stokers sleeping off their labors and catching pneumonia or the wabbling back and forth of the mighty steerage gear from which the steerage got its name. There was no library, no entertainments of any kind.

I. Of the Landed Gentry

Somewhere I picked up a paper-backed copy of Dumas's *Three Musketeers*. If your taste for literature is jaded you may bring it back to life by reading a good book, or any book, after four days of solitary seasickness in the cellar of a ship. *The Three Musketeers* may not be the finest novel ever written, but I am afraid to read it again for fear of finding out that it isn't.

On a calm evening we came into New York. Its sky line, topped by the Singer Tower, was a dream come true. We tied up to the water front, somewhere in sight of a shining clockface in a tower, and the trueborn Americans went happily and noisily ashore. Then they pulled the ship ten feet away from the dock so that no immigrant might dodge Ellis Island. Until late I sat on the rail, watching the ferryboats scuttle about like agitated water bugs, and marveled that this was America.

Next morning they herded us on a tender and took us to Ellis Island. Someday I hope to return there and bust somebody on the nose for old time's sake. We were there at early morning. They locked us in cages, created by wire fencings reaching from ceiling to floor, with not much to sit upon but our baggage. Nothing happened until noon. Then we were marched by a wicket window, told to lay down fifty cents and rewarded with a box lunch of sandwiches, coffee and an apple. Then we went back to our cages.

At late afternoon we were marched again past a variety of inspectors, hastily vaccinated and investigated for eye diseases. Men in uniform asked personal questions. I admitted I was neither anarchist, nihilist nor polygamist. I said I had $15 in my pocket and a place to go. The man in uniform thought that $15 wasn't much but let me through.

So at nightfall they set me ashore at Jersey City, clutching the ticket to Philadelphia which was part of my paid transatlantic fare of $35. I also carried one heavy bag, a cane and a genuine carpetbag. And I was eighteen years old.

I think of it sometimes when one of the boys develops restless notions at what strikes me as an infantile age. Fourteen, for instance, which was the age at which I gave up schooling and earned wages at a full-time job. Or eighteen, when I left the land of my fathers for a strange and unknown country, probably inhabited by wild Indians and buffaloes.

And I think sometimes, too, that the pangs and unpleasantnesses of

My Own Four Walls

emigration and Ellis Island may have their place in the making of an American. There is reason to believe that being born, in the first place, is a painful affair. It may be well that the barriers between Europe and America, in those days, were not too easily hurdled.

The inconsequential immigrant of 1908, one of millions, had no serious thought of staying here. He planned to pick up the loose ends of an education and eventually go back where he came from. He had not the slightest intention of teaching in an American school or working on the staff of an American newspaper.

But a lesson of life, if you live long enough to learn it, is that one thing leads to another in the most surprising fashion. Another is that planning a course and career before you are twenty is usually a waste of time. The road forks too often, there are too many detours and the future has no maps.

In October 1908 I certainly had no notion I should ever be invited to enroll myself as a member of the American landed gentry, of British ancestry, with the privilege of purchasing the book for a trifling $20.

Now I am an American, not merely by land ownership and the paying of taxes but also by immigration, naturalization, matrimony and the parentage of twelve young Americans of assorted sizes and sexes. If these qualifications do not make me an American, the thing can't be done.

II

Where's the Fire?

Had you been born in England on June 29, 1890, you would have been thrilled to be appointed, twenty-five years later, as second lieutenant of a truly rural fire company in the neighborhood of Philadelphia, Pa. The place is called by the Welsh name of Bryn Athyn, meaning a hill of harmony and cohesion, which is something to live up to. Smallest borough of Pennsylvania, it stands sixteen miles from the big city's crossroads, four miles from city limits on one side and with wide-open country on the other.

The full title was Second Lieutenant in Charge of Hose and Nozzles. Fire Chief Fred Finkeldey hung it on me. Both of us were teachers in the local academy and considered competent to command the loyal service of the community's young man power. Ours was a goodly company, subsequently famous in local fire-fighting circles for wearing army tin hats while on active service, and the title of Second Lieutenant in Charge of Hose and Nozzles was nothing to sneeze at.

So it seemed, anyway, until I found out that after a fire in the rural areas around Philadelphia it is the second lieutenant's unhappy job to see to it that the hose is dried, rolled and heaved back into the fire truck. And if the other boys go home to breakfast, he can do it himself.

In my British boyhood days I had known firemen mainly as splendid creatures in brass helmets who hung about theaters and concert halls and enforced "No Smoking" signs. At rare intervals, the English being a non-incendiary nation, they rushed to fires behind galloping horses in a cloud of smoke and cinders.

A volunteer fireman's life in the United States, fifteen years later, was less splendid but more fun. When appointed Second Lieutenant in Charge

My Own Four Walls

of Hose and Nozzles I selected my second-best pair of working trousers, laid them handily by the bedside and prayed nightly for a fire. The company had been organized and equipped a little too late for the finest fire ever seen in our neighborhood, which I helped to extinguish with a half-inch garden hose. The fire went out, finally, when there was nothing left to burn, as fires usually do in the country regions. After that the community organized a volunteer brigade, bought a pumper and half a mile of hose and was ready for business.

The Second Lieutenant in Charge of Hose and Nozzles slept fitfully for months after, hard by his second-best working trousers, waiting for the midnight welkin to ring with news of a fire.

I was schoolteaching at the time but sometimes went to Philadelphia for an afternoon's dissipation at Keith's Theatre. On the way home one evening Herbert Johnson, the cartoonist, shared a seat on the Newtown local. That afternoon he had spoken with his wife by telephone, who told him a thunderstorm was raging and the fire whistle blowing.

II. Where's the Fire?

It was tragedy to have missed the first real fire since I became Second Lieutenant in Charge of Hose and Nozzles. It turned out that I had not altogether missed it.

The fire, of course, was in the house where I lived in a second-floor apartment with a wife and incipient family. The lightning bolt had hit a tall tulip tree, skipped to the roof and buried itself in a mattress stored in the attic, where it soon smothered to death.

The volunteer fire brigade had come and gone. From high-pressure hoses it had poured tons of dirty water into the burning building, most of it into our living room on the second-floor front. From there the water went into the hall, down the stairs and out the front door again.

Willing hands had salvaged all movable furniture and effects from the flames, which never got out of the attic. Carefully they had carried out the piano and left it on the lawn in the pouring rain. A vast sideboard, filled with nothing in particular, had been miraculously moved intact down the rickety rear steps. A china closet stored with our landlady's best crockery and glasses had been tilted forward and carried out wrong side up, so that everything within went down to cureless ruin.

Somebody had dared the roaring torrent on the stairs to rescue the loose head of a newel post. Similar heroism saved a bunch of green bananas. Our store of clean towels had been tossed out of the second-floor window and the table lamp after them.

Approximately everything else in the building, except the smoldering mattress, had been carried to the shelter of neighbors' porches. At which point the volunteer fire brigade went home.

In something less than two weeks, as the only able-bodied man in the vicinity, I had moved it all back again and was slightly less enthusiastic about volunteer fire brigades.

But I still slept beside the second-best trousers, waiting for the still alarm and a sporting chance of reaching the firehouse before all the rubber boots were gone. For the rubber boots, in those days, were the real reward of membership in a volunteer fire company. To stalk fearlessly and officially in hip boots among glowing embers and roaring water gave a man a chance to throw his weight around. But there were not enough boots and first come was first served and the firehouse was atop a long hill, so that too many times I attended fires in sneakers or bedroom slippers.

My Own Four Walls

The next fire of any consequence was on the afternoon of Christmas Eve in 1916, when the Worthington barn caught fire and made a thorough job of burning to bare walls and a pile of baked potatoes. We spoke of it as the Worthington place because Ben Worthington lived there, but Tom Shriver owned and rented it. The potatoes were Newt Branin's, ten tons of them.

Newt Branin owned Huntingdon Valley's leading and only butcher shop. In early Benedict days I did some of the shopping there and remember Newt as a ponderous person who had lived so long among fresh meat that he resembled his own merchandise. He also made a solemn ceremony of putting on a fur-lined overcoat before entering his butcher's icebox.

That may be why he lived so long. I have a valued souvenir of his passing. At a decent interval after the funeral there was held a public sale of his effects, or some of them, including a fairly prehistoric Packard car in excellent condition. It was said that Newt liked to own the car but rarely rode in it. We bought the car and found it in fine mechanical shape, spotless within and without. One reason was a beautiful brass cuspidor, apparently regarded as essential equipment for the passenger department. The cuspidor went with the car. The car returned to original chaos long years ago, but I still have the cuspidor.

Newt's horses and cows were removed safely from the blazing barn, but nothing could be done about his hay and potatoes. Not much more could be done about the fire, but we fought it to the finish. It nearly finished me, anyway.

Partly this could be blamed on the rubber boots. It was bitter cold and the water froze where it fell from the hose. You have missed a magnificent sensation of perilous uncertainty if you have never tried to hold a struggling hose while standing in rubber boots on sheet ice. That dangerous duty fell to the Second Lieutenant in Charge of Hose and Nozzles, and I would have murdered anybody trying to take it from me.

A hose with five or six hundred pounds of water pressure inside it and trying to get out is about as manageable as a man-eating python. Professional firemen know how to break its proud spirit, but I didn't. Venturing close to the blazing inferno for better aim at the potatoes, I stepped too far on the ice-coated sward. The hose leaped with glee, threw me with a neat half nelson, hit me in the rear with full stream and sent me spinning

II. Where's the Fire?

across the ice. With a final contemptuous flick of its tail it filled my boots with ice water. Fellow firemen rescued me and I went home to thaw out.

The barn burned cheerfully to the ground. It was one of the oldest and least beautiful buildings in the village, and the prevailing opinion was that its burning was no great loss. There was some concern for saving the near-by farmhouse and outbuildings, in which I took no part. I was too busy warming my frozen feet and sipping hot whisky and water.

For two winters and a summer the bare walls of the ruined barn stood gaunt against the sky. Charred rubbish and wreckage lay deep where the lowing herd once greeted the morning milking. The farmhouse forgot its ancient purpose and was tenanted by transient families of working folk. Rarely I saw the place, since it lay beyond the village limits.

In the early spring of 1918 our living quarters on the second floor became overcrowded for comfort, with three children kicking the place to pieces and endeavoring to fall out of windows and off balconies. At a social affair in Philadelphia I overheard the rumor that the farmhouse and thirty-six acres around it had a new owner, who would sell in whole or part. Sight unseen, I telephoned him that I would buy the farmhouse and a little land around it.

It is now incredible that I could buy anything in the spring of 1918. My pedagogical salary had started at $50 per month in 1914 and reluctantly doubled in four years. But during those years there was a war, and the American government persuaded the people to pay for a slice of it by purchase of Liberty bonds. These were obtainable by easy payments, which were usually anything else but, and as the war neared its end I found myself richer by $1000 worth of negotiable bonds. They were particularly negotiable because men with money were grabbing all they could get of non-taxable securities. At that time taxes meant nothing in my young life and I sold.

I think it was old John D. Rockefeller who said that the first step toward fortune is to save $1000. You can't do it on $50 a month with prospects of advancement unless somebody throws in a war and unless you are a schoolteacher with a full three months' vacation every summer in which to work at something else. But when the crisis and opportunity came the $1000 was in hand.

Asking price for the property, including one acre of land, was $3000, one third in cash and the rest on mortgage. It seemed fair enough to me. But kind friends of greater financial experience cast doubts on the proposed transaction. They hinted that the house was a wreck and the land a liability. They suggested that an expert viewing committee should inspect the property and do a little bargaining on my behalf.

No early American farmhouse in the last stages of decay and dissolution was ever honored by visit of a more distinguished viewing committee. Two of the three were millionaires, or near enough for all practical purposes. The other was their financial secretary or something, my friend Ed Bostock.

Nowadays Ed Bostock is one of my favorite people, but in the early spring of 1918 I thought him a suspicious sourpuss. He took one look at my potential property and pointed out that its only "improvements" consisted of a man-power pump over a probably polluted well. He sneered at the hand-wrought shingles on the roof and said they would leak. He promised that the children would fall down the steep stairs, which they subsequently did. He complained that the wavy window glass gave a horribly distorted view of the outdoors and that to walk across the living-room floor was to invite seasickness.

In the cellar, a gloomy hole with less than headroom between dirt floor and joists, he whipped out a pocketknife and attacked the timbers. At that time termites had not been invented. He said that the joists were weak with dry rot. In some cases their ends had melted into nothingness, leaving fine holes for rats to nest in, and the east end of the house was standing on the coalbin.

I now think that termites did it. That cellar, in its original condition, was never dry enough to suffer from dry rot. I have heard, though, that termites never start to tear houses down until encroaching civilization has wiped out the woods and forests where they prefer to feed on fallen trees. Probably the picnic parties were partly responsible. After a few years of community picnics you can't find enough dry timber in the woods to boil a small coffeepot.

When Ed was done with the house it was a shameful shambles. The unfortunate owner stood by, dropping the price by $50 and $100 at a time. Ed showed no signs of weakening but pointed out that the alleged acre probably included half the dirt road that ran in front of the house. The

II. Where's the Fire?

owner hastily agreed to throw in more land. "Including the barn," said Ed sternly. The owner winced but agreed to the barn. The barn, after all, was a wreck and eyesore.

The final price was $2500. The deed was done and signed. I owned a house.

III

O Rare Ben Yerkes!

Title to the house, the barn, the carriage house, the chicken yard and one and one thirtieth acres of land was transferred on August 16, 1918, by testimony of the deed. By that time I had found out that when you buy a property for $2500 that isn't the whole financial story. There are mysterious expenses for title searches, writing of mortgages and registration thereof. At the time I suspected all this was something of a legal racket, and now I'm fairly sure of it.

In 1918 I took somebody's word for it that the title had been searched to its roots and found safe and sound. Years later I searched it myself, with some assistance from a Philadelphia bank and trust company that goes in for that kind of thing. We had grown fond of the house and curious concerning its past history and ownership. When it was bought there was no knowing when it was built, except from a wooden date board so weatherworn that nobody could be sure whether it said 1835 or 1882. It was not likely to be 1882, for no house could be tired out so thoroughly by a trifling life of thirty-six years. So we took it for 1835 and told the neighbors so.

Later we decided that it should have been 1832, and now the old date board is replaced with a record in cement which will last longer than the house.

The written story of the property goes back to 1792, which was about when my great-grandfather was born. In that year George Washington was re-elected President of the United States, so it must have been some time ago.

Since then the land has known nearly a score of owners. Its original acreage has been several times divided or swallowed up by a neighbor farm. It was sold twice, at least, at sheriff's sale and has figured in three

III. O Rare Ben Yerkes!

wills, one of them fought through the courts and involving an insane asylum.

There were ten acres of it, "more or less," on May 5, 1792, but no mention of a house. But on April 2, 1832, John Webster and Mercy, his wife, sold the ten acres, "be the same more or less," together with a "certain stone messuage and tenement," to Benjamin Yerkes, wheelwright, who paid $700 for the whole works. I am glad I didn't know it in 1918 or it might have taken the edge and savor from my $2500 bargain.

Modern deeds to real estate, including mine, define the limits of the property in tiresome detail, but the old-timers got the same effect with hit-or-miss measurements. The record of 1792 refers to "premises situate in Upper Moreland Township, beginning at an oak stump." Not a word about which side of the oak stump or whether the stump would still be there when neighbors got to quarreling over property lines. But it was still there forty years later, when Benjamin Yerkes bought the ten acres. Other landmarks mentioned in the original deed are the mill formerly of Joshua Morris, a stone on the property of Thomas Austin and "a line of land formerly of Samuel Boutcher." When Ben bought it there was also a road, "a certain road laid out from Lady Washington Inn to Addis's Mill." The mill still stands and a road still makes a beeline, the shortest distance between two points, from the mill to what used to be the Lady Washington Inn.

They must have met often at the Lady Washington when the day's milling and wheelwrighting were done. It was only a half mile over the hill for Ben Yerkes, and wheelwrighting is a thirsty business. Others there, whose names are found in these musty documents, were Harvey Kintzing, Henry Wynkoop and Amos Addis, and there was news enough to talk about.

"Have you heard the new song?" asked Ben. "They say 'twas written by Samuel Francis Smith, he being a Baptist minister in Massachusetts. 'My Country, 'Tis of Thee,' they are calling it, and the tune was taken from England's anthem. Why it should be, I cannot say."

"The country has trouble coming," said Amos Addis. "Did you note that the nation's debt, this first of the year, was $24,322,235? It's a great sum, and our children and children's children will carry its burden on their shoulders."

My Own Four Walls

"That comes of the greed of the politicians," remarked Henry Wynkoop. "So much was admitted on January 25 in the Senate. 'To the victors belong the spoils,' said Senator Marcy of New York, and that's where our money goes."

"But this is a powerful and rich nation," argued Harvey Kintzing, "and it is my belief it will yet grow more so. We have come far since '76, but there is a great way to go. I read that next November will be opened the new railroad between Philadelphia and Harrisburg, and the wagons will no longer be mired in the mud when only two miles away from a merry evening at Rising Sun Tavern. For, mark my words, they will carry our farm stuff by the railway and bring back coal the same way.

"They are beginning, too, a railway between Boston and Worcester, which are said to be proper towns, though too far from Philadelphia. And only last year was finished the highway to Pittsburgh, with 177 miles of canals on the way. 'Tis a wonderful age in which we live. And one of my wife's cousins has gone far beyond the frontier and built the first house in Iowa, though I wonder why anybody should live so far from good company and in daily danger of wild beasts and Indians."

Amos Addis shook his head gloomily. "No good can come of it," he said. "So much rushing around for no sensible reason. Over in New York they are to open soon a street railroad. 'Twill run from City Hall to Fourteenth Street and frighten a lot of good horseflesh out of its wits, I wouldn't wonder. And the cholera has come from New Orleans and is bad in Philadelphia."

"It's the fault of the Democrats," said Ben Yerkes. "President Andrew Jackson has much to answer for, and may do so next November."

"You'll vote for Henry Clay, I take it," said Wynkoop. "There's a young man is speaking for him and running himself for the Legislature of Illinois. Lincoln is his name and his first name Abraham, I think, and though he's but twenty-three years of age he seems a likely man."

"Did you hear that Charles Carroll died?" asked Amos.

"And who was he?" asked Wynkoop.

"He was the last man to sign the Declaration of Independence," explained Amos. "And sometimes I have wondered what good the Declaration did for us in Moreland Township. We are free people, 'tis true, but there's little work for the mill and no money in it."

III. O Rare Ben Yerkes!

"Business will mend," said the hopeful Kintzing. "Meantime great things come to pass, if you would note them. They have begun a new college at Easton and named it for General Lafayette, and another at Gettysburg. A bold man by name of Henry Schoolcraft has pushed far north into Minnesota and found where the great Mississippi has its beginning. A new journal of news has started in New York and is called the *Globe*, but many wonder will it last long. There are few can read, and fewer have time for it."

"How like you your new home, Ben?" asked Henry Wynkoop. "It looks a solid piece of work."

"The kitchen fireplace will not draw well," said Yerkes, "and the roof shingles are not the best. But with proper care it should serve my lifetime, or as long as I care to live in it. It troubles me, though, that I paid too much for it."

"It was $700, I hear," said Harvey Kintzing. "A great deal of money, indeed, but John Webster was always known to drive a hard bargain."

There was much more they may have talked about in 1832, when the day's work was over and a stiff drink of whisky was to be had for five cents. Perhaps they were still speaking of Sam Patch, who had lately destroyed himself magnificently by jumping the Genesee Falls at Rochester, N.Y., "in the presence of a great assembly." Perhaps they were wondering about galvanized iron, only recently invented, or mourning the fact that bricks were now being made by machinery and leaving idle hands among brickmakers.

It is likely that John Webster had no machine-made bricks and had never heard of galvanized iron. His little house was built of field stone and hand-hewn lumber and he sold it, for some reason, to Ben Yerkes, wheelwright by trade, who lived there many years and his son after him.

I have met Mr Yerkes only in the spirit but know something about him. He must have been a good wheelwright and worked hard at his craft. When he wrote his will, in 1851, his ten acres had increased to thirty-two acres seventy-one perches, "more or less," with barns and other buildings, all of which he bequeathed to his wife Sarah. He also left her $100, "as soon as convenient." So much property was wealth, in a modest degree, and Ben Yerkes gained it by the sweat of his brow and minding his own business.

My Own Four Walls

Not much of this we knew when we surveyed our property on the morning after its purchase, suffering a slight financial hang-over from having shot away our total savings on a pig in a poke. First reaction was the realization that you mustn't poke a pig too hard or the pig may fall down.

In the cold gray dawn we noted that the walls of the house were out of whack and a third of the windows broken. A low-roofed wing was leaning away from the rest of the building and daylight leaking through the crack. There were joists beneath the first floor, but not enough of them, and the floor rolled under traffic like the deck of a ship.

I called in a carpenter to admire the wide boards of the floors, fastened down with hand-wrought nails. He was a young man with undimmed illusions and ambitions but would only talk of matched long-leaf pine to be nailed irrevocably over the historic surface.

That was the time when restoration of early American farmhouses was an architectural fad and Joe Hergesheimer was writing a book about it. The book had a lot to say about wide floor boards of seasoned pine, waiting only the touch of the sympathetic hand to make their patina obvious to the retina. I mentioned it to the carpenter. He said these weren't the right kind of floor boards.

Later I believed it. There are still sections of floor in the house that are imperturbably naked after applications of fifty-seven varieties of oil, paint and varnish. There are also some patches of white paint, probably put on by Ben Yerkes, which could only be removed by dynamite.

We were pleased to find the house full of fireplaces; not so pleased to note that most of them were boarded up, papered over and equipped with connections for stovepipes. Even then we suspected that the fireplaces smoked.

The house needed water, light and heat when we walked into it. My wife, even then, was one of these modern women who won't wash dishes in well water or clean lamp chimneys. I shall not anticipate the painful details of wiring and piping which made the house habitable but will merely mention that if you ever try to insinuate a heating and lighting system into a house of eighteen-inch stone walls and solid six-inch timber partitions you are in for more trouble than Joe Hergesheimer ever wrote about.

III. O Rare Ben Yerkes!

Outside the house was an acre of land and a lot of dirt, most of it in the wrong place. Nobody has ever explained why the dirt is always in the wrong place when you buy a house, but it is. Right away I wanted a terrace where my predecessors preferred a ditch, and a rock garden on the site of the ancestral chicken house. I wanted a sunken garden, but it was obvious that to get it I would have to sink it. During our first summer of residence I spent days and weeks moving dirt. On a fine afternoon I would don my working trousers and attack one of the numerous mounds that dotted my acre like tumuli on the Western plains. I would work till nightfall and break my back and the shovel. And when I hopefully surveyed the undesired hump it looked as though a mouse had been nibbling at it.

There was also the barn, two hundred tons of stone piled on end and held together by iron-hard lime mortar. In two years since its burning it had crumbled and been torn down until it looked like a cross between the ruins of Pompeii and the League of Nations. Children and centipedes were climbing over it, and burned and rotting wood lay cluttered beneath it. A well lurked within it, and at the bottom of the well were two dead rabbits.

My Own Four Walls

The garden, in the spring of 1918, scarce deserved the name. Neglect and old age had nearly obliterated it. There were nettles on the road bank, poison ivy in the shrubbery, owls and bats in the maple trees. Within the house there were rats in the cellar and spiders in the walls. Over the whole business brooded a first mortgage for $1500.

This was not the "certain stone messuage and tenement" which Ben Yerkes bought with pride in 1832 and inhabited until he died. And I seemed to hear John Webster, who may have built the house, speaking to Mercy, his wife. "There she is, my dear, and she'll stand three-score years and ten, with proper care, but not much longer."

IV

In the Pennypack Valley

When John Webster built his house he picked the place for it wisely, putting it comfortably in the shoulder of a hill and hard by running water. Not quite close enough to his springhouse for my taste, for its doorless and windowless ruin was off the lot when they laid out my acre. And I have no envy of the housewives who must have traveled two hundred yards for cool milk and butter when the house was younger.

Loss of the springhouse was a sore point, and eventually I put myself to work to make another. Marshall Fuller, then a schoolboy in need of pocket money, helped me dig the hole and build it, and that was my first initiation into the ancient art of masonry. The springhouse looks the part. Its erratic and mossy walls might well have been laid a century ago. Its broad steps of stone go fourteen feet underground and get nowhere. The error was that we built it in rainy season and thought we had reached the spring when we were still two feet short of it.

It never mattered much. The water wasn't fit to drink, though it used to be when Ben Yerkes worked the pump handle above the well. So the springhouse is not much more than a hole in the ground, roofed with concrete and two feet of earth and entered under an arch of masonry. It looks nice and has been useful for storing apples and growing mushrooms. In its dankest depths, at the bottom of the steps, the temperature never rises above 56 degrees or drops to freezing point.

And it will be an elegant bombproof shelter, I suppose, whenever somebody tries to lay waste the Pennypack Valley.

The Pennypack winds a quarter mile away and accounts for the old mill, which has had a dozen names since it was built, depending on who owned it. It was a gristmill, but the Pennypack is better known for its

My Own Four Walls

paper mills of the past. They gave their name to a crossroads railroad station two miles away and there must have been half a dozen of them. Now they are only heaps of stone, hidden in poison ivy.

This Pennypack Valley is not yet so far from the primitive, and you may find along its banks many relics of easier and harder times. They may be no more than a broken barn wall. But the barn and the house which belonged to it were built out of the soil on which they stood. So was my house, which is of random field stone because field stone was the farmer's pestilential nuisance when Pennsylvania was young.

They were prodigal with stone, these handy men of a hundred years ago. There is enough in my buried well to build foundations for a modern bungalow, and I have one chimney which must weigh twenty tons. The stone came out of the farm, and a century of farming didn't get it all. There is plenty left in the garden around the house, and the frost still heaves it out to turn the edge of garden tools.

IV. In the Pennypack Valley

Houses and barns like that of Ben Yerkes lie casually in all corners of the hills along the Pennypack Valley. A native likeness and simplicity of design are stamped upon them, partly by the necessities that environed their building and in part, perhaps, by the hand of some journeyman mason or builder who worked through the valley. The simplest plan for the bulk of the house—a pair of stout chimneys, a lower wing for kitchen or storeroom, small dormers in the pitched roof, unused shutters flanking the windows of small panes. Unpretentious enough, yet fitting rightly into the elbow of the hill, under the arch of maple and spotted buttonwood.

"How did they do it?" I asked an architect who had built splendid homes and stately churches.

He sighed with some envy. "No plans or blueprints," he said. "No specifications, no contracts. A sketch with a carpenter's pencil on a scrap of paper, I suppose, and the rest was in the builder's eye and hands. They laid that wall by squinting at it and by the feel of it. Down in the valley of the creek there are a dozen barns and houses built that way, and after ten years of training and practice I couldn't design the outside of them much better."

Not many of them are left now, for some are improved and restored out of character and others have gone down for lack of occupancy. There are some grand stones still to be found in their ruins. Doorsills of flat rock from the creek bed and occasionally the chipped slab once built into the kitchen wall to serve as sink on the inside and drain on the outside. On the farms there are also millstones, serving now for round steps or flower stands, some in a single mighty slab of granite and others pieced ingeniously into a ring of iron bands.

I could never get myself a millstone, so made the best of it with a grindstone. At an auction sale across the creek it sold for a nickel, which is cheap enough for three feet of grindstone. Only difficulty with that much grindstone is that it costs $1.50 to have it hauled home. And when you get it home you have no clear idea what you are going to do with it.

A kind friend came along and gave me an antique Italian sundial of hammered brass. It was a beautiful sundial, and you can never tell when you will need to know the time while picking Japanese beetles off the hollyhocks. So I built a concrete pedestal for the grindstone, laid it flat thereon and attached the sundial, pointing it accurately toward high noon.

My Own Four Walls

At twelve o'clock, Eastern Standard Time, the sundial was right to the second. From then on something went wrong with the works. Days of trial with a stop watch discovered that only once a day could the sundial tell the true time, which was at midday. Other times you might as well call the telephone operator.

Solution to this mystery was finally found in the fact that the sundial was designed to tell time on a wall, not a grindstone. Standing upright, it could tell the time within five minutes; flat on its back, it knew nothing about it. I pondered moving it to a sunny wall but pondered too long. An itinerant junkman came along seeking what he might devour, found nobody home, ripped the sundial from the grindstone and went on his wicked way.

Had John Webster lived a little closer to the creek he might have built my house of ironstone, or whatever it is that weathers in pleasant browns and yellows. But the bulk of the hills is granite. Most of it is cold gray and blue, almost too hard for road building. A little of it is colorful, and some of it went into the building of the Bryn Athyn Cathedral on the hill.

All through the Pennypack Valley are found small quarries, but nature has been kind to their age and disuse and has dressed them again in green and taken the rough edge from their scars. The creek road winds from one to the next and is not much of a road. But it winds as the creek winds, through the hills and woods, arched by trees and with the grass creeping close to the track of wheels and hoofs. It is friendly neighbor to the stream, and they jog along together to the edge of city life where both are prisoned and lost.

Few come through except on horse or foot, for the road is still of loose rock and sand. Floods spread clear over it when the valley is suddenly filled with water from a hundred swollen springs. A better road could hardly take it, and this is the proper companion for the banks of a country creek.

It is a road to wander along without regard to time or destination, a road to be learned and loved. Its graces and small surprises are infinite. The gossiping stream on one side, the quiet hills on the other; the ancient fences of timber split and hewn, the patched patterns of sunshine and shadow. Here is no grandeur or splendor, but the intimate enjoyment of small pictures and the company of memories of human use.

IV. In the Pennypack Valley

Some wretched road commissioner will mend the road someday and die in his sins for it. For though flat country is bettered by the hand of man, he should leave valley and stream alone. Here running water has chosen its own way; chosen it long ago with due respect to the rocks and hills, taking always the easiest, quietest path. The woods have grown and died and lived again along these wandering banks; immemorial generations of birds and flowers have found a home. The confusion of growing things is here made fair and ordered by the sparkling thread of water that is their life and reason. Pick and shovel, hatchet and saw, tape and transit would give for these a poor substitute.

Between the loveliest countryside in this corner of Pennsylvania the Pennypack finds its way. Old rocks lie in its path, listening through centuries to the trifling babble of water on their sides. Trees hem it in, losing at last their foothold on the crumbling bank, to lie half submerged until wind and water make away with them. In rocky glens small waterfalls throw back the sunlight; in wider stretches the spring clouds are mirrored or fallen leaves dapple the silent water. Summer or winter, night or day, faint mystery of age and youth and life eternally renewed encompasses the valley, granting constant charm and comfort to all with eyes to see.

Not long ago there were covered bridges through the valley, spanning the wandering creek to permit the impatient line of the Reading Railroad, which started out this way for New York but changed its mind at Newtown. One by one they have burned or broken, these wooden sheds with their mighty timbers and hooded roofs, and their passing has taken some of the character from the scene.

The old stone bridges are still with us and likely to stay, judging by their masonry. And there are some crossings by steppingstone, to be found by the footpaths that lead to them and bearing small hazards of slippery rock and uncertain balance.

There were dams when the mills were running, but they went down before spring thaws and summer storms, and it was nobody's business to restore them. So the stream is shallow almost everywhere and there are few swimming holes. In places its bed is steep and the water noisy, curling in eddy and cascade over the polished rocks. And only a mile or two below us it loses suddenly its playful ways and becomes sedate and sensible and, in a fashion, middle-aged. It grows fat and lazy, spreads out between easier

My Own Four Walls

banks and finds its way at last through open fields to the great Delaware and the sea.

It is good to live by the Pennypack, though long ago it ended its tale of useful labor and traffic. It still has its share in the pleasanter purposes of the neighborhood. Romance has its moments in the shadow of its trees and on its quiet waters. There are small paths that lead nowhere but are traveled not a little. In spring and summer there is the quiet passage of canoes along the creek, chaperoned by croaking bullfrogs.

Even in winter the creek does its bit to make life worth living. There may be skating by day or in the patterned moonlight, with a roaring fire on the bank for comfort of cold feet. An immigrant Englishman, in 1908, was taken there to be taught to skate by his fellow students. In southern England, where I lived until eighteen, ice is a comparative novelty, rarity and exception to the rule. So when I came to this country in 1908 I could not skate. I still can't skate.

But when I got here and went to school I yearned to shed as rapidly as possible my alien habits and inadequacies. They told me it was nothing at all to learn to skate. So I borrowed skates one bright winter afternoon and went down to the Pennypack.

I found it little trouble to put on the skates and felt encouraged and hopeful. Two kind schoolmates, likewise on skates, guided me to the midst of the ice. There they found it necessary to call in a third to support me from the rear, but at last I assumed a reasonably vertical position and was ready to cast off. So I thanked my friends politely and assured them that all would be well. They left me there.

At this awkward moment one of my feet decided to go home. The other was more venturesome and started away down the creek. Nothing I could do at the moment seemed to bring them to any sort of agreement, so I sat down on the ice to think the matter over.

With some difficulty they picked me up again, and this time I managed to assert the mastery of mind over matter and keep my feet in harmonious relationship. Unfortunately I was unable to keep up with them as they dashed away down the creek and almost at once resumed a recumbent position. On the third attempt I did better. I fell down, it is true, but managed to execute a figure eight, two sixes and a seven by sliding all over the ice on the collar button of my spine.

IV. In the Pennypack Valley

So I spent the rest of the evening tending the fire by the creekside and the rest of the winter catching up on my reading.

Almost as painful was my first acquaintance with the gentle American pastime of sledding. There was a girl with whom I would have preferred to sit by a friendly log fire and talk of many things. She preferred to go sledding. The hills of Pennypack Valley were glazed with an icy crust, following a freak of weather described in the old verse:

> *First it rained and then it snew,*
> *Then it friz and then it thew,*
> *And then it friz again.*

I wore borrowed rubbers, and the icy surface was just at the condition where it sometimes supported me and sometimes let me through, cutting the rubbers and sorely afflicting my soul. We climbed a long, smooth hill, while I wrestled between the desire to walk upright like a man and the temptation to get down on all fours and make better progress. The girl, with that irritating assurance characteristic of American womanhood, got along very nicely. It was my manly prerogative to haul the sled after me as we clambered up the hill.

We reached at last the very edge of the hilltop, after a struggle which would have done credit to Admiral Byrd in the Antarctic. The girl waited ahead for the beginning of a glorious ride down the frozen valley. At that moment, for no good reason whatever, I lost hold of the sled. It started off on its own and slid easily and rapidly clear down to the other end of the county.

Since those days I have never been on a skate and do not care for sledding.

V

On Armistice Day, 1918

There is a prevalent opinion that the builders of early America were more painstaking and honest than their modern equivalent. The fact is that some were and many were not. The high reputation of ancient craftsmen rests partly on the fact that their good work survived while the bad went to pieces. So when you buy a farmhouse with a century of history under its roof you may expect it to be built well enough to stand a century more.

Not only American monuments foster this fallacy of the worthiness of all that is old and well seasoned. Probably there were more old churches and cathedrals of Europe that fell down, burned down or were torn down than have lasted till now for the admiration of American tourists. The wreckage of some can still be seen at Glastonbury, three miles from my British birthplace, and at many other places in England. Many have vanished altogether or are memorialized by a meaningless heap of stone.

Some started to fall apart and were patched together again. The curious inverted arches of Wells Cathedral in Somerset, now claimed as one of the building's outstanding beauties, were put there to hold the tower up. The famous lantern of Ely was an afterthought of alterations and repairs. Near my native village the lovely tower of St Cuthbert's is on the wrong end of the church. It was originally on the right end but fell down.

John Webster was not a conscientious and careful builder, or else he could not afford to be. Let it be remembered, however, that he was not building for posterity and the twentieth century. He was building the simplest sort of farmhouse with whatever lay to hand.

V. On Armistice Day, 1918

So he set his cellar joists two feet on center instead of a substantial sixteen inches. He made his plaster with soft sand and lime, and not much lime. He hewed roof rafters from green oak logs, not caring that they might twist and split. He pegged his timbers to save hand-wrought nails and the pegs shrank and fell out. He built stairs too steep and chimney flues too narrow. He allowed little space for a decent coat closet or linen cupboard and none at all for a bathroom. He designed fireplaces so that they would certainly smoke, and his successors boarded them up and heated the house with chunk and coal stoves.

But he did not spare stone, of which he had plenty, so the house is cool in summer and warm enough in winter and its windowsills are nearly two feet deep. And they are framed in white pine, which was cheap wood a century ago though not now.

In moments of pessimistic reminiscence I sometimes wonder whether it would have been wiser to tear away the whole house except the walls and build a new one inside them. And that, for a fact, is what most people do who say they are "restoring" an old American farmhouse.

We had no such plans in 1918 nor the money to pay for them. We could not even undertake the mending of the house's more obvious mistakes and weaknesses. I tried it once, during the early restoration period, and repented of it. The main roof was thatched with hand-split shingles, a full yard long and half an inch thick at the butt, green with moss and soft as punk. Amazingly they did not leak much, but in a reckless moment I decided to replace them.

The shingles came off and revealed the fact that the rafters were in sad state. So were the chimneys, and one was leaking smoke below the roof line. Patching the chimney discovered that much of the wall was crumbling. Putting in new rafters brought down part of the ceiling in the attic. At which point we quit, hastily put on a new roof and tried to forget it.

But when we bought the place the immediate problem of essential repairs and improvements was met by a construction loan, an ingenious device whereby a bank pays the contractor's bills in hopeful expectation that the place will be worth that much when finished.

I was advised to employ a team of architects. Both are dead now and both were young then and probably learned better when they were older.

My Own Four Walls

It was their misguided idea to revise an 1832 farmhouse with additions and alterations in English cottage style. The kitchen they planned was cute but had no proper place in Ben Yerkes' old homestead. And I made the grievous mistake of allowing them to build it over the well.

Now I wish fervently that I had the well as a garden centerpiece, but in 1918 the well was a headache. It was eighteen feet deep and held four feet of water, plenty to drown six or eight small children. Something had to be done with the well.

But you can't do anything with a well. You can't pull the well out of its hole, and the well's masonry and mortar were too tough to take apart. You can't sell a well to somebody who wants a well. You can't even give it away to the Salvation Army.

So we lidded over the well and built a kitchen above it with a wooden floor, and in a few years the floor died of dampness and decay and began to subside into the excavation. Which I still believe and will maintain was the fault of architects who should have known better.

They should have known better, too, than to have built a modern kitchen with no possible place to put a kitchen cabinet and with rough-plastered walls to collect dust and cobwebs. They should have had a sympathetic thought for the feminine passion for closet space. They should have known that women don't like small windowpanes if they have to wash them.

I fluttered feebly around while they planned and plotted, but got no more attention than I deserved. It was then, and may be now, a prime principle of the architectural profession that nobody knows so little about building a house as the man and woman who have to live in it. The professional arrogance of the architect is not offensive but tolerantly paternal. The architect knows best. Like fun he does.

This was my initiation, too, into the wiles and wickedness of the building trades when working on a cut-price contract. I did not know it then but found out years later, to my sorrow, that there is no such thing as cheap building. There is low-price building, but it is not cheap. It is not cheap when the roof begins to leak and the kitchen floor collapses.

There is very little you can do about it, either, if trapped in a cut-price contract, specifications or no specifications. Any time you turn your back the contractor starts cutting corners. I caught him at it once. Coming

V. On Armistice Day, 1918

unexpectedly home from school, I found a man mixing mortar for the chimney. Even to my untutored eye the sand he was using looked strangely like the stuff that had been dug out of the cellar excavations. And that is what it was, to be seasoned with a little cement and called mortar, or grout, if you care to be technical.

The architects came to my riot call and admitted that the contractor was building my chimney with mud. They told him he shouldn't and he said he wouldn't. Lately I have found out that he did. A thin skin of honest mortar has weathered away and the mud is leaking miserably and messily down the wall. It will do so until I can afford to take the chimney apart and put it together again properly.

Another long-standing grievance against all building contractors is that they cannot guess within six weeks when their work will be done. So they say it will be done six weeks before it will be.

The result was that in early September, a week before school opened, we loaded our lares and penates on a one-horse wagon, piled the three kids in the baby coach and moved in before the carpenters, plumbers, painters, electricians and laborers had moved out. The house was fit for use in only a haphazard degree. There was running water on the second floor but none on the first. There were no windows or doors in the dining room. And for a week or two a flock of chickens sat down to meals with us.

There was, in fact, no finished floor to the dining room, and table and chairs were perched perilously on loose boards laid on the joists. And sleeping late in the house at that time was a hazardous and embarrassing business. You might wake to find a carpenter under the bed, an electrician behind the door. You could count on a plumber in the bathroom at any time. Wasps, flies and hornets were everywhere. A friendly chicken laid an egg in the washbasket one morning. A neighbor's cat had kittens in the dining-room fireplace.

By late October the job was sufficiently finished, however, and we planned a housewarming. Just in time we got the bathroom done. This was a small room that was once a bedroom, for it appears that the previous inhabitants had no use for bathrooms. Presumably they bathed beneath the pump, and for other purposes there was an edifice beneath the apple tree. No better or more enduring structure was ever built on the property. It was much too good to waste, and I wondered long what to do with it.

My Own Four Walls

The final solution, and a good one, was to take a two-man saw and cut it in half. That was more than twenty-two years ago, and the upper half would still make a good dog kennel except that we have no dog. It has been highly regarded as a doll's house and still serves to store small tools and flowerpots.

Inserting a bathtub in the bathroom was no trifling problem. We thought for some time that we should have to invent a sectional bathtub or a rubber one that could turn a corner to get upstairs, for the front stairs of the house are steep as a ladder and scant of headroom. Finally we compromised with necessity by tearing out the side of the house and elevating the plumbing with a block and tackle.

The housewarming was arranged, at random, for the evening of November 11, 1918. Friends came from far and near, and I cannot remember how we got so many into the house. A small fire blazed in the living-room fireplace, a much bigger one in the cavernous affair that served the dining room, once the farmhouse kitchen. I had managed to get my way with the architects about the kitchen. It had been a low-ceilinged and gloomy hole, with its floor laid flat on a rubble of lime and mud. Above was a little attic, evidently used for storing apples, for remnants of the apples were still there.

I ripped out the attic and left the room with a high peaked ceiling, raised the floor a foot and rebuilt the hearth of the fireplace with flat stones. The fireplace, of course, was boarded over when we found it. Back of it was an old-time oven, built into the wall. A rough-hewn timber supported the face of the fireplace, six feet across and four feet deep.

We built a great fire in it, which turned out to be a good idea. Subsequently we learned that anything less than a bonfire in the dining-room fireplace smoked us out of house and home. A big fire created such a terrific draft that the smoke had no choice except to climb the chimney.

So friends and neighbors came to the party and rejoiced with us, admiring and envying our magnificent fireplace. There was a small ceremony of dedication and considerable conviviality, with a witch's cauldron of mulled wine on the hearth for all comers. You mull wine, by the way, by heating a poker red hot and plunging it into the hot wine, and I cannot swear that it makes any difference to the ultimate consumer.

There was a mood of rejoicing and thankfulness over the party that

V. On Armistice Day, 1918

had nothing to do with the fact that we owned a house at last. The armistice of the First World War had been signed. And we believed then, not knowing any better and hoping for the best, that there would never be another.

After midnight the guests went home and there was a little time for musing by the dying embers of the fire, watching its sparks flicker and flare and vanish like the fond dreams of men who build houses and dwell in them. And it seemed then, and still does, that a home must be built about a fire of warmth and cheer and friendliness, or else it is not worth building.

Such meditations were rudely interrupted when the sparks began to travel the wrong way. They were coming down the chimney. For a while this seemed no more than a curious phenomenon, to be expected in a resurrected farmhouse, but the matter turned serious when chunks of flaming wood began to fall on the hearth. It occurred to me, finally, that the chimney was on fire.

The contractor had rebuilt the chimney and raised it a few feet for better draft. To save trouble for his masons he had built the extension around a wooden form. Dried out by summer drought and the heat of the dedicatory fire, the form was blazing to cinders and ashes. There was thin snow on the ground and no great danger, but I watched and waited till it burned out. It would be poor fun to spend six months and $3500 of borrowed money making over a farmhouse and have it become a bonfire on Armistice Day.

VI

Be the Same More or Less

A comforting statement appears in "An Essay on Original Land Titles in Philadelphia," by Lawrence Lewis, Jr., published in 1880. "The most scrupulous mind may rest satisfied that the titles derived from the Commonwealth since 1779 may be conscientiously owned and enjoyed."

Since the first deed covering the land which includes my acre is dated August 15, 1752, its title and my conscience should both be clear. Careful reading of this and other documents makes me not so sure.

Anybody owning a piece of land in Pennsylvania, or anywhere else, should sit down on it sometimes and reflect that he has a small slice of history beneath him. Somewhat to the discredit of our civilization, much of its record lies in the history of land ownership. And if I knew all about the land at my back door, its various possessors and vicissitudes, I should be much wiser in American history than I am.

Except for the remote possibility of earthquakes, the land has always been precisely where it is today. But scores have claimed to own it, even in the comparatively brief period since the discovery of America. Before that I doubt anybody bothered to own it.

I doubt the Indians bothered to own it, but they didn't mind selling it. By my reading of the ancient records, various Indians sold it to any white sucker who happened to come along. On June 23, 1683, four smart redskins, named Essepenaiki, Swanpees, Okittarickon and Wessapoak, disposed of "all their land laying betwixt Pemmapecka and Neshemineh Creeks and all along upon Neshemineh Creek and backward of the same, and to run two days' journey with a horse back into the country as the

VI. Be the Same More or Less

said river doth go." The Pemmapecka, as you may imagine, is now the Pennypack, and there are other ways of spelling it. It has been called the Penepek, Penepec, Penepak and Pennepeck, and if you can invent any other way of spelling it you can probably count on a historical precedent.

Other Indians sold the same land in 1684, 1685 and 1697, which strongly suggests that the plundering of the poor aborigines was not entirely a one-sided proposition.

Title searches pay no attention to the Indians and are satisfied to find their way back to William Penn. It is a pleasure to live on land once belonging to William Penn, granted and given to him by King Charles II. One reason is that my maternal grandmother was a Penn, and it is a family legend that I am thereby related to the first proprietor of Pennsylvania.

It is in strange contrast to the customs of today that King Charles gave Penn a large part of Pennsylvania and invited him, in turn, to give it away to his friends, neighbors and relatives. To Nicholas Moore, a lawyer from England, he seems to have given 9815 acres, which is why I now live in Moreland Township, formerly called the Manor of Moorland. Nicholas had a daughter named Mary, and Mary married the runaway son of an English preacher, Elias Keach, whose historic distinction is that he pretended to be a preacher himself but broke into tears and confessed his crime in the middle of his first sermon. And Mr Keach is among those present in the gallant company of those who have bought and sold my little property.

Their names are too many to mention and their relationships too complicated. But the deeds which record their trading are entertaining to read.

By 1752 there were left only eleven acres and twenty perches of the great Manor of Moorland, which sold for thirty-three pounds. In 1792 the price was up to one hundred and fifty pounds, and witnesses to the transaction were Anthony Yerkes and Samuel Ayres. Anthony, I suppose, was ancestor to the Benjamin who bought the place in 1832. Samuel Ayres was probably grandfather to Elizabeth Ayres who is now remembered in the name of the next-door village of Bethayres, Pa.

Elsewhere in this narrative it is claimed that my house was built in the year 1832. Quite likely it wasn't, and perhaps it doesn't matter much. It was said of Voltaire, by Madame du Deffand, "What more would you

My Own Four Walls

have? He has invented history." So have I, by fixing a date for a house which might have been built in 1832, in 1814 or even sooner.

For the deed of December 7, 1814, by which John Fisher and Elizabeth his wife sold ten acres, "be the same more or less," to Robert Manson for the odd sum of $355.60 "lawful money of the United States of America," mentions a messuage, and a messuage is "a dwelling-house, especially one with its adjacent outbuildings, garden, curtilage, etc." Robert Manson sold it again in the following year to John Webster for $522.50. And it was John Webster and Mercy, his wife, who sold it for $700 to Benjamin Yerkes.

There is no doubt that the land is the identical ten acres, be the same more or less. But who built the house the deeds do not say, nor how much of a house it was. I have invented history in assuming that John Webster did it in 1832, and my date stone to that effect is set too firmly in the wall to be taken down. Yet the house may be thirty years older.

The deed of 1752 describes the land as "beginning at a Black Oak Tree being Corner of Thomas Austin's land in the line of Samuel Boutcher's Land." There is a note of sadness in the statement of "An Essay on the History and Nature of Original Titles to Land in the Province and State of Pennsylvania," published by Charles Huston in 1849, that "it seems to have been taken for granted that trees would stand forever. They die as well as men; they are cut down, and blown down, and killed by fire running through the woods; so that at this day there are many tracts of ten miles square in the older counties in which there is not to be found a single tree marked at the time when the first survey was made."

The Black Oak of 1752 served the purpose of a cornerstone for nearly a century. An "oak stump" is mentioned in 1814, 1815 and 1832. But when Ben Yerkes died and his land and messuage were sold, in 1865, the stump was gone.

In some of these deeds there are curiosities of the purchase price. Christian Snyder bought the land and some more, in 1865, for $4501.57. Before that, on April 1, 1841, Charles Ayres had sold Ben Yerkes twenty-two acres and seventy-one perches, "be the same more or less," for the extremely precise and fractional price of "One thousand one hundred and thirty-two Dollars eighteen and three quarter cents lawfull money of the United States." It would have been simpler, perhaps, to make the price an even $1132, "be the same more or less."

VI. Be the Same More or Less

From a number of historians and antiquarians I was unable to learn how Charles Ayres could make change of a quarter cent in the currency of the middle nineteenth century. Not even from experts of the Land Title Bank and Trust Company, whose assistance in tracking my title to its roots is gratefully acknowledged. It was my country banker, Israel Hallowell, who suggested a simple and reasonable explanation for the eighteen and three quarter cents.

A quarter, or twenty-five cents, was fairly big money in those days. Half a quarter was one "bit," and I am told that you could cut a coin in half and use both pieces for currency. And half a bit would be six and a quarter cents. So a little mental arithmetic settles it that eighteen and three quarter cents were a bit and a half, which was near enough to even money.

Through the mists of time and the befuddling language of the law it is clear that many changes have come upon land since William Penn was giving it away in generous chunks, sometimes asking a red rose, acorn, peppercorn or white perch per annum as quitrent. At first it was wild land so plentiful that 9815 acres of it were no more than a small token of esteem between friends and partners in politics. Then it became land to be cleared and plowed and planted. Its price went up from $15 an acre to $45; then to $50 and $70. But it was still land paying its way.

Thirty-five acres sold for $9000 on January 3, 1902, which would be about $257 an acre. The price was a sign of the times. The property was no longer land; it was real estate. And only sixteen years later it was sliced to pieces, divided into building lots, and a little more than an acre, including its dilapidated messuage, tenement, outbuildings and curtilage, was worth $2500.

I hope it was, anyway. I hope it is worth $16,000, the sum of its mortgages, today. I hope it is worth even more than that. But by overmuch study of these faded documents I come to the confused opinion that whatever it is really worth is only whatever it is good for, be the same more or less.

Two bits make a quarter, and five and a half yards are one rod, pole or perch. The latter I learned by rote in my early English schooldays and wondered, in childish innocence, why five and a half yards should make a fishing trip. But my deeds make it clear that a perch is not necessarily a fish. It was once a vital unit of measurement in laying out land and deeding it.

The dimensions of those days were in acres and perches, for the perch is a square measurement as well as a linear. The length of property lines was so many perches, and a few feet one way or the other didn't matter. Anything less than five and a half yards was covered sufficiently by the phrase "be the same more or less."

But when land became real estate the surveyors began to figure in feet and inches and fractions thereof. Evidence is a deed of recent date, covering a small swap of land with my next-door neighbor, Kenneth Synnestvedt.

He wanted a better roadway to his back door and I wanted a slice of his wood lot. It was proposed to make even exchange, trade or barter of two pieces of property, similar in size though violently different in shape. It sounds simple enough, but before we were finished with it we wished we hadn't started. The legal operations wore out one able-bodied lawyer. A viewing committee, representing the respective mortgagees of the two properties, came and inspected the land, walked all over it, studied cornerstones and fence lines and looked at maps and documents. Total expenses of the transaction were enormous, more than the land was worth for any conceivable purpose.

The legal documents dealing with the transfer are not much more intelligible to the lay mind than one of Dr Einstein's blueprints of the created universe, though they cover less territory. They cover, in fact, only 2,722.463 square feet, "be the same more or less." And when the job was done and documented the land lay exactly where it was before and neither of us was a nickel's worth better off than before, though the lawyer was.

There was this difference, though, that my rectangle of real estate has developed a kind of bunion on its southern frontier while my neighbor's has acquired a curve in its northwest corner. It takes an amazing lot of language to say so in the deed of transfer. Description of the properties makes no mention of simple rods, poles or perches. The distances are definite down to the infinitesimal fractions. My line, running westward, extends for "nineteen and three hundred sixty-three thousandths feet." And the document is full of fractional angles and dimensions, including a mysterious forty-six thousandths of an inch which is mentioned repeatedly.

VI. Be the Same More or Less

Somewhere between the two properties is a point which must be forty-six thousandths of an inch from some other point, or else generations yet unborn may quarrel and go to law about it. I have often wished I could locate that spot and sit down and look at it. Perhaps some tiny violet, born to blush unseen, woke up there on the morning of March 24, 1937, to find itself with a new master, while the seedling poison-ivy plant beside it belonged to the party of the second part. If so, I probably got the poison ivy and my neighbor got the violet.

In preliminary discussion of the transaction we shifted the tentative frontiers back and forth in friendly dispute over ownership of an ancient apple tree. It was a rather lamentable argument, because the apple tree was there before either of the contending parties was born. Sometimes, indeed, the whole business of real estate seems reprehensible and ridiculous. For it is something of a shame to slice up a broad sweep of hillside into little pieces and call them thine and mine.

Not very long ago, after all, this was a fertile farm of broad and uncertain acreage, but now it looks on paper like a crazy-quilt pattern drawn by a doodler waiting for a telephone call. Once there were sixty acres surrounding my house, and now there are one and one thirtieth acres and forty-six thousandths of an inch.

This may be progress, in the suburban interpretation of the term, but we may sit awhile in the shade of the old apple tree and mourn the more spacious past. It will never be so again, but this was once an ample apple orchard, and beyond was a broad cornfield and beyond that a meadow where mushrooms grew plentifully in season. Some farmer of former days could drive horse and wagon half a mile without leaving his land, though now I can hardly change my mind without trespassing on the forty-six thousandths of an inch which belongs to my neighbor. And there were six acres of woodland in the valley, more or less, and how much more or less didn't matter. There were the spring and stream and swamp, and no argument as to whom the frogs and water cress belonged.

Souvenirs of those times turn up whenever I get busy with pick and shovel. Down to the edge of his land the farmer hauled the stones he found in his fields, and some of them were honeys. He built his house and barn with them and doorsteps and dry walls with the bigger ones. It needed no little acreage to grow such a crop of field stones and boulders.

My Own Four Walls

A nice chunk of stone lies along the line where the visiting committee walked with deeds and maps and mortgages. I have hesitated, so far, to move it. As near as I can figure it, the tremendously important forty-six thousandths of an inch is underneath it.

The mistake we made, my neighbor and I, was in swapping our land by lawful means and procedures, all 2722 feet and a fraction of it, be the same more or less by forty-six thousandths of an inch. The wiser plan would have been to have risen early some fine morning and moved it with shovel and wheelbarrow.

VII

Stretching a Shoestring

Some years ago a friend looked over the house and garden and listened to part of their history. "It seems to me," he said, "that you've done wonders on a very short shoestring."

I liked the compliment but cannot properly take it at face value. It is true that the place cost me $2500 in the rough and raw and is now valued by the local tax assessor at ten times that much. Until lately it supported two mortgages of $8000 apiece. The outbuildings which I have restored and rebuilt for rental bring in a monthly income of $110, which would be more if I were a tough landlord.

And yet I have never, until lately, had any real money of my own to spend on the place.

Part of the answer to this financial riddle is that the surfboard rider gets a lot of credit which belongs to the wave which is going his way. I could have sat on my acre for twenty years and twiddled my thumbs, and it would have doubled in value under me. The land lying fornenst my own, not yet inhabited, is hopefully priced by it owner at $5000 an acre. Having a better frontage, mine must be worth more through no fault of my own.

It now seems likely that a lot of people made a grave mistake, after the First World War, in buying stocks and bonds instead of land. Their holdings went sky-high while they sneered at my struggling landlordship. They all had cars, partly paid for, while we were pushing baby carriages. They read the stock-market news while we looked for basement bargains in wallpaper, house paint and garden tools.

They also figured endlessly on the backs of envelopes, planning to call quits when their accounts showed a balance of $100,000. Then they would buy land, build houses and barns and inhabit them.

My Own Four Walls

The depression arrived, roughly speaking, when their balances with the brokerage houses were $92,000, not quite enough to satisfy. None of them had $92,000, of course. In the years preceding 1929 everybody was making money but nobody had any. The money was supposed to be in stocks and bonds, in safe-deposit boxes, in Wall Street or somewhere. It turned out, unhappily, that it wasn't anywhere.

So they all fell off the band wagon at once and landed in the slough of despond. I couldn't take the tumble, because I had no place to fall from. And I learned then and hope to remember for future reference that the only people who don't lose a shirt when an economic house of cards collapses are those who have no shirt to lose.

It is more important, probably, that when the bottom fell out of everything else I still had solid earth under my feet, not merely the remains of a financial rainbow round my shoulder. It may be a law of economics, for all I know, that when all other values crumble and evaporate the worth of land will be the last thing left.

But buying land is a gamble too, and luck plays its part in the game. It was by better luck than management, if not by blind necessity, that I bought my real estate in the right place.

The community of Bryn Athyn, in eastern Pennsylvania, is not an easy place to explain. It was founded in 1894 by a group of Philadelphia Swedenborgians who liked the idea of living in the country and minding their own business. They desired a place where they could establish their own school, build their own church and interpret their faith in terms of civil, social and religious life.

For this purpose their richest member, the late John Pitcairn, bought a considerable acreage in Moreland Township, Montgomery County, and sold some of it again, piece by piece, to those who could afford to leave Philadelphia and build new homes in the country. Then it was not easy. Then known as Alnwick Grove, in honor of a small amusement park on the Pennypack Creek, the site of Bryn Athyn was on a toll turnpike and a one-track railroad. It was all farmland, scattered with a few ancient houses and barns.

But Bryn Athyn grew and flourished. It is the scholarly report of our local historian, Dr William Whitehead, that no other religious community has lasted so long in the United States and kept strictly to its purpose.

VII. Stretching a Shoestring

Others have become industrialized or have opened their gates to all and sundry. But Bryn Athyn, now housing nearly a thousand people, is still ninety-seven per cent Swedenborgian.

Partly this is due to the centralizing and stabilizing influence of its schools, supplying the needs of all ages from kindergarten to collegiate degree, in which I studied six years and taught for eleven. Education is the community's only industry, aside from some architectural studios established for the building of the Bryn Athyn Cathedral.

The Academy of the New Church, collective name for the entire institution, supplies all services of a public school and college but is private in the degree that youngsters must be baptized into the Swedenborgian faith to be eligible for enrollment. Mainly they are Bryn Athyn boys and girls, some of them the third generation to study here. Others come from all parts of the country and from many foreign lands.

The schools would not integrate the community so completely if they were not dedicated to the teaching of a single faith and philosophy. It may be said, therefore, that the theory and practice of Swedenborgian faith are the foundations of Bryn Athyn and the reason for its successful survival. Otherwise, by now, this would be no more than a pleasant suburb of Philadelphia or might have succumbed long ago to change and decay.

Instead it may now be called one of the county's most completely organized and self-sufficient communities. Since 1916 it has been a borough, its affairs administered by unpaid citizens of high and low degree. For a dozen years or more I have myself been president of its school board, an almost honorary office with no emoluments whatever. Boroughs must have school boards, with duly elected officers, but this one has no school that owes direct allegiance to the state. A few youngsters not eligible to attend the Swedenborgian Academy and Elementary School are enrolled in the Moreland Township schools and paid for pro rata. But more than three hundred get their teaching in the red-roofed buildings atop the hill and can stay there, if they please, from kindergarten to college degree.

Bryn Athyn has its own clubs, its boys' organization, its taproom, corner store and swimming pool.

It has also its church, the cathedral headquarters of one section of the world-wide sect of Swedenborgians. Undoubtedly the preachings within its Gothic walls have profound effect on the life and character of the community. But so does the building itself.

Since 1914, when its foundation stone was laid on June 19, the church and tower on the hill have imperceptibly molded the ways and mores of those living near them. It must have been so in medieval times, when a cathedral church or abbey laid kindly shadow on a whole countryside. There was beauty before their eyes in those distant days, but more than beauty. Any good and honest craftsman might have a hand in the building of his church. The least laborer might learn, by good example, the difference between good and bad handiwork. He might know something, merely by living in their daily presence, of many ecclesiastical arts and crafts. He might build his own humble home better and more beautifully in imitation of magnificent architecture.

The medieval cathedral, moreover, found much work for men, women and children to do. Bryn Athyn is not in the least medieval, but many of its people, particularly the young ones, find something to do in service to the cathedral on the hill. They sing in its choir, play in its orchestra, are guides and ushers. They have watched its building, still unfinished. Many have been baptized there, married there, will be buried from there. Daily before their eyes, not as a pleasing spectacle for tourists but as part of their lives, is a great work of art and architecture, reckoned among the finest in America.

So the tower on the hill casts a long and searching shadow. To the cathedral the people of Bryn Athyn are likely to turn on all great and moving occasions. When news of the armistice came, in 1918, it was there they went by common consent to spread the flags of victory and join in service of thanksgiving. There they have gathered for hundreds of other ceremonies and celebrations.

It is still too soon to reckon the depth and breadth of the influences radiating from the tower on the hill. But I am conscious they have done much to direct my own housebuilding. An outward and visible sign of it is the fact that certain arches and doorways on my acre are of Gothic shape. They got that way because I purchased, many years ago, several wagonloads of scrap lumber from the church building and found among them the forms used for the cathedral's Gothic windows. But it is more important that the slow growth of the cathedral made me aware of walls, of steps, of mounting levels and balanced masses. And others may have

VII. Stretching a Shoestring

been similarly influenced, for the excellence of suburban architecture in Bryn Athyn is well above the average. It is a community of pleasant homes with land to spare, well shaded with good trees, most of its homes looking from some window toward the tower on the hill.

All this may be necessary to explain why the law of supply and demand has been generous to realty values in Bryn Athyn and its vicinity. A lot of Swedenborgians and some other people want to live in Bryn Athyn. Their desire to do so puts up the price, a phenomenon by no means exclusive to a religious community.

So Ben Yerkes' farmhouse and the acre surrounding it, then beyond borough limits, were really worth more than I paid for them in 1918. My special luck was that I saw them first, badly needing a place to live and with $1000 to lay on the line.

The borough proceeded to spread out and surround me. A reluctant gas company laid mains past my door and still charges the highest possible prices to pay for them. Neighbors built nice houses up and down the road, to the unearned increment of my own property. The Reading Railroad ran more and faster trains, though its management is still unable to imagine any reason why a countryman should wish to stay in Philadelphia later than 11:40 p.m. The old turnpike turned honest, the tollgates came down, the highway was straightened and surfaced with concrete. Land values went up for miles around.

This was a sort of inflation, I suppose, and I hadn't much to do with it. I did have something to do with the financial kiteflying which brought me, finally, into apprehensive possession of first and second mortgages totaling $16,000. Somehow the property must now be worth that much, at least, or no banks or building associations would loan the money to carry it. Though during the depths of the depression it was told me, in a banker's confidence, that the only good mortgage was one which paid six per cent semiannually and no questions asked. Mine managed somehow to do so, though a lot of others went to the wall.

Had anybody mentioned $16,000 in the spring of 1918 I would have fainted from fright. The total estate from which my acre was cut, something like thirty-six acres, had just sold for $12,000. But the gentleman who bought it needed to sell some of it pretty quick to pay for it, and that is where I came in.

My Own Four Walls

We began by paying $1000 in cash money and borrowing the other $1500 of the purchase price on mortgage. Next step was a construction loan of $2000 for the purpose of essential repairs and to make the place habitable. When the job was done this went on the mortgage.

This might have been a good place to stop and take it easy. But my friend and neighbor, Will Cooper, seriously needed a place to live and believed that Ben Yerkes' wheelwright shop could be made over for the purpose. Will is what is known as a "handy man around the house." He could use the tools of half a dozen trades and suggested that I should finance a few fundamental alterations to the wheelwright's shop and he would do the rest, in consideration of a nominal rent for a period of years.

It was a sound idea, except that Will got himself a new job and another place to live and left me with half a house on my hands.

This might have been my financial Waterloo in a less friendly community. At that time bankers were going into epileptic fits at the mere mention of lending money. I tried peddling my proposition to half a dozen institutions, allegedly in the business of making loans to deserving citizens, and they would have none of it.

But Bryn Athyn is unique in more ways than one. Its democracy is of the spirit and its charity is of the heart. Naming no names, it was a kindly individual who came to the rescue with a loan of $3500 on second mortgage, its principal to be reduced by semiannual payments.

Later I learned that the mortgage was never recorded. Later still he asked me to meet him at the train as he left on a trip to Europe. As he caught the train on the run he handed me an envelope, and I didn't see him again for four months. Inside was the mortgage.

There is a reason for mentioning this deed of kindness, aside from the compulsion of honest confession that I didn't swing this thing without help.

It was once the way of American life that men with money did much more with it than spend it and pay taxes. Many still do. They regard their wealth with a sense of responsibility to their friends, relatives and even their neighbors in need.

Their discreet lending and giving served to cushion the shocks of many past depressions. Their help started or sustained many men in sound

VII. Stretching a Shoestring

ventures and was wasted in many others. Sometimes their timely aid saved a man's pride, often his possessions, perhaps his life.

They still do it. But the difference today is that government tries and promises to do it. Washington is the place whence all blessings flow, and the gentle rain of government handouts falls alike on the just and unjust. So some quality of neighborliness has gone out of American life, for better or worse. Nor can I much blame the man of means today who swears at high taxes and resolves to let the government play the role of fairy godfather, friend in need, patron of the arts and plain sucker for a hard-luck story.

I like to believe that my friend regarded his gift of $3500 as an investment in personal credit. Banks will lend money on that basis in good times but not in bad. Economic thunderstorms curdle their milk of human kindness, which is not much better than skimmed milk in the best of times.

After this windfall of friendship the country's economic condition took a turn for the better and the banks loosened up. With the wheelwright's shop built into a house and inhabited, I was able to increase my borrowings, based on the improved value of the property. For the first time in its ninety-odd years of history the house boasted both a first and second mortgage, duly recorded at Norristown.

I did it again, by a complicated process of refinancing, when it seemed right and proper to rebuild the ruined barn into a two-story apartment house. That was at the height of the boom, when any kind of financial hocus-pocus seemed right and proper and it was practically impossible to lay a losing bet. Everything was on the up and up, so why not borrow another $5000?

Sometimes since then, when having a little tenant trouble, I have cordially wished that I hadn't.

I repeat that it is the wave, not the rider, that carries the surfboard ahead on a high tide. In the years before 1929 the tide was all going one way. A financial wizard was anybody who could lay hands on a little money and hire it out to Wall Street. The same principle applied, in less degree, to buying lands and building houses.

My one and only experience with the market proved the point. My esteemed father-in-law, Colonel John A. Wells, told me I should positively buy a chunk of Hudson and Manhattan preferred and make myself some

My Own Four Walls

money. I had no money nor the slightest idea what a preferred Hudson and Manhattan might be. This, apparently, did not matter.

The colonel said he would lend me $600 to buy Hudson and Manhattan preferred. What's more, he would see to the buying and selling of the same. A few weeks later he dropped in to hand over my $200 profit. It was that easy.

At the time it seemed too good to be true. Actually it was too good to last, which is nearly the whole story of the market crash of 1929. Fortunately the $200 didn't go to my financial head. It went to a new outside kitchen and refrigerator room, most of which I built myself.

I have neglected until now the fact that for twenty-two years, man and boy, I have been wrestling in person with the wrack and ruin of an old farmhouse and trying to make something out of it. How much, in terms of money, my labors have added to its market value I cannot calculate. Nobody could, not even an expert on income-tax deductions for alterations and repairs, improvements, depreciations and obsolescence.

For money, in the past twenty-two years, has not stayed put. When we started housekeeping eggs were twenty cents a dozen, and the price seemed high enough. A dozen eggs are still a dozen eggs, but twenty cents will never be the same again.

Ben Yerkes bought my house and ten acres for $700; I paid $2500 for the house and one acre: today I would think twice, if not three times, before settling for $30,000. But an acre of land is no more or less that it used to be.

I know I have borrowed about $20,000 and I presume I have spent it. The increase, including the use of the house and lot for twenty-two years, came from somewhere else. Some of it is part and parcel of rising realty values in the borough of Bryn Athyn. The rest of it is the work of my hands, and thereby hangs this tale.

VIII

My House Is Haunted

It may be doubted whether a convincing ghost story was ever written. Plenty have tried to write one, but the result is either a plausible impossibility or else the ghost turns out to be a fake.

There is Lytton's yarn, for example, of the invisible creature which dropped on a sleeper's chest like a nightmare in the flesh. They captured it, struggling horribly and invisibly, and it died in its bonds. Title of the story is "What Was It?" Well, we're all listening. What was it?

Other ghost yarns blow up in the last chapter or paragraph. The ghost is only the villainous butler in sheet and pillowcase or a bloodhound with phosphorus on his whiskers. In which case the yarn is no ghost story.

The problem is like that of staging the ghost in *Hamlet*. The ghost may be a flickering light or shadow on the castle wall, which fools nobody. Or else he is an actor who had ham and eggs for breakfast.

Yet a house like mine should be haunted by a few ghosts, preferably nice ones, and so it is. They do not clank chains in the attic, partly because there is no attic. They do not groan in the cellar. I never meet them making nocturnal rounds in search of their skeletons.

Seated one evening at dinner, twenty years ago, we did hear a ghostly groan from the cellar. It was not precisely a groan but rather the shuddering sigh of a sleeping giant. I turned pale to hear it, thinking that the furnace flue had fallen down again and spilled soot all over the cellar.

But I found the flue in place and the cellar floor clean. I could not even discover any unusual evidence that the house was collapsing. In next morning's newspapers we read that it was no ghost that had haunted our evening meal. It was only an earthquake. That's what they said, anyway,

My Own Four Walls

though scientists admitted there was no trace of it on their seismographs. But hundreds of my neighbors heard it and some swore they felt it.

I still have hopes of finding a skeleton around the place somewhere. Or else at least a jug of fine corn liquor laid away by some former owner and forgotten. We almost had it two years ago, when I was laying second-hand bricks over the dirt floor of the cellar. In a corner was a thick layer of lime plaster; beneath it a neat frame of rotted timbers, eight inches thick, making a two-foot square.

The wood was rotted to dust and splinters. Beneath it the ground rang hollow to the pick. I dug a foot deep and found nothing. One of the boys came down to call me to dinner and thirty minutes later was waist-deep in the hole, hard on the heels of hidden treasure.

At three feet the pick struck something which gave forth a dull metallic thud. By turns we dug furiously and found it. It was a chunk of field stone. Only that and nothing more. So we filled the hole, laid the bricks, and I am still looking for the skeleton, the pot of gold or the jug of corn liquor.

When we had bought our house in 1918 we knew very soon that it was haunted. As spring worked its way into summer we found it habited by quiet ghosts of garden lovers who had planted it around with lilac and peonies and lilies of the valley and "pie plant"—plain rhubarb to you, perhaps. It is a pleasant thing to find lilies and lilac in a garden you have not yet learned to call your own. Somebody put them there, a long time ago. Later in the year came tall clumps of golden glow and cider apples from a gnarled and neglected tree.

All these hinted of daytime ghosts, still hanging around the work of their hands. Tread of their feet was plain in what was left of the pasture and apple orchard, where the grass grew differently along the beaten tracks of old-time traffic. There was one to the ruined springhouse and another led over the hill, direct toward the Lady Washington Inn, and the short cut to the mill could still be traced through the brier thicket beyond the barn.

But a better ghost was found when we stripped from the living room a wallpaper of poisonous red roses about the size of six-pound cabbages. We repaired and painted the plastered wall, and out through the new paint leaped the plain outlines of a grandfather's clock. Several times since then

VIII. My House Is Haunted

the wall has been painted or papered. The ghost of the clock is still there. It came there, I suppose, because for half a century the clock was oiled or waxed and polished as it stood at the foot of the stairs and ticked the years away. It stood there while three generations lived and died. Then came strangers, and the clock went away but left its mark.

Now I have found the clock again, still ticking in a house not far away. Maybe it will come home someday, though its present owners will not part with it. Its old place against the wall is waiting.

We saw or heard no more ghosts until the second spring. On a May morning I heard a vast buzzing and humming, also the indignant swearing of a farmer from over the hill. "My bees," he told me. "I want my bees." The bees, by then, were beginning to hang in a clump from the highest corner of the house, which seemed a silly location for a bee to go into business.

I said he could have his bees. The bees were a cloud in the air and a squirming mass on the cornice, thirty feet away. So the farmer swore some more and went away without them.

All summer and fall the bees buzzed about and collected honey and laid it away in the roof for a rainy day. They bothered us very little, except when a lazy child sat down on a busy bee, and I bothered them not at all. But when the fall faded I called on Professor Vinet and told him about my bees.

Professor Vinet teaches French in the Bryn Athyn school, a thankless task which has earned him the enduring gratitude and affection of all his students. I still recall our first acquaintance, dating from when I entered his class with my English accent still thick upon me. We differed somewhat as to how, why and whether the British won the Battle of Waterloo.

Professor Vinet was and is a great teacher, a classical scholar who speaks Latin with a French accent and a farmer and beekeeper who believes that honey will cure all the ills that flesh is heir to. He said the bees were shutting up shop for the winter and now was the time to swipe their honey.

So I set up a scaffold, and he climbed up with gloves and veil and took a few shingles from the roof, speaking softly but emphatically in French to any bee that tried to argue with him. From under the roof he took twenty-eight pounds of honeycomb, some of it nearly black with age but most of it eatable. For many years, he said, the bees had known of this

My Own Four Walls

cozy corner in the cornice. I left a loophole for them when I mended the roof, but they never came back.

So we found the house haunted by bees and gardeners and a grandfather's clock, but that was not all.

Later I discovered that the able-bodied Americans who built the house a century before were still hanging around. As I messed about the place I was aware of their presence, standing around with ethereal hands in ectoplasmic pockets and keeping an amused eye on me. And I soon found that they were running me and my house, though decently dead and buried a long time back.

When I moved into my relic of early Americana I was a typically helpless specimen of civilized mankind. I could earn a living but not by working for it with hands and tools. I couldn't harness a horse, steer a plow, swing an ax or milk a cow. I had none of the ancient and honorable handicrafts at my finger tips. I could read and write but hardly hit a nail with a hammer. I could handle a telephone receiver but not a plastering trowel.

The house and its builders took me gently but firmly in hand and proceeded to teach me what a young house owner should know.

It could be done only because the house itself approved. I could live a lifetime without learning anything in a modern and sleazy house, slicked up with machine-cut trim, tiled bathrooms, chromium kitchen fixtures and a host to alleged labor-saving devices. If anything breaks in that kind of house, it needs an expert to mend it. If anything goes wrong or falls apart, it can be repaired only by the expensive ministrations of unionized mechanics and artisans.

But a house made like mine, by handy men with simple tools and materials, can be mended in the same way and by the same kind of man and no uncritical eye will know the difference.

It has taken me twenty years, but I have learned the use of the tools needed to build a house a century go. They were the hammer and saw, chisel and gouge, hatchet and adze, level and straight edge, plane and punch and a piece of string. There were also the mason's and plasterer's trowels. The rest were luxuries, if they knew them at all, and I doubt the ghosts who haunt my house possessed them.

Perhaps it is the house, possibly it is the ghosts who have trained my civilized and clumsy fingers to the aboriginal skills of plain car-

VIII. My House Is Haunted

pentry, masonry and bricklaying. It is certainly the ghosts who urge me on.

"Fix it yourself," they whisper. "Do it yourself. You've as much brains as a bricklayer and your time is your own. Don't let anybody tell you different. If you want a brick floor to your cellar, lay it yourself. If your garden needs a wall, build it yourself. Build it the way we did, by rule of thumb and the looks of it. There's nothing to it that a man of common sense can't learn."

A lot of times I have looked across my shoulder, while busy in the garden or workshop, to see who was standing by. Nobody was there. Nobody is there, I persuade myself, when there is a rustling of footsteps in the woods beyond the garden or a creaking and shuffling overhead in an empty room. Ben Yerkes is long dead and decently buried. So are all his friends and kinsmen. They were sound citizens and good workmen, but they cannot haunt a house.

Well, why not? If there is another world hereafter, it must have its foothold here. And if a man is immortal, some of his heartstrings may be forever tied to the home where he lived and labored, hoped and suffered. Perhaps this means only that the house he builds in a better world is somewhat in the image and likeness of the one he inhabited here. But it may mean that sometimes he wearies of the bright skies of heaven and wants to see a sunset across the Pennypack, tinting the tops of his own silver maple trees.

I would worry about my house, I think, if I glanced across astral space and saw a fumbler meddling with it. Ben Yerkes, or some other spirit, may be properly concerned that I shall not spoil his handiwork or forget his craftsmanship. So sometimes he stands at my elbow and whispers good advice. Sometimes I am not alone as I stroll solitary at night in the garden or what is left of the orchard. "A man may be known by the company he keeps," said Cervantes, and mine is the sturdy company of men who worked with their hands for what they had, and made it increase and prosper.

So the ghosts had their way and the old farmhouse still looks the part, though changed beyond knowledge of those who once lived in it. Two of them came to call some years ago, two elderly sisters who said they had lived here a long time. They were troubled that we had torn away

My Own Four Walls

partitions, added wings and totally rerouted the household traffic. They sought in vain for traces of their garden and went away sadly.

But what has happened to the house has not changed its character much, despite concessions to modern convenience and comfort. Two homemade fireplaces and a lot of brickwork and plastering of my handiwork are much the same as John Webster and Ben Yerkes would have done them. My stonework and carpentry are not much worse or better than theirs. I like to imagine that they looked on, in the spirit, while I worked at them.

These ghosts of mine were good workmen in their time, if not skilled craftsmen in all the building trades. Their land's increase came of work—work with hands and tools. The house's betterment came of work, and I do not doubt that this was a better house in 1882 than fifty years sooner, when Ben Yerkes bought it. Ben and his son, their heirs and assigns, made it so by their handiwork. Never by a neat turn in the stock market and the hiring of architects, contractors and builders, but by their sweat and labor.

Are we, who live here now, getting back to where they started a century ago? Sometimes it seems so. Lately came cold comfort from the local tax assessor, who says my property is more valuable than when he last put a price on it. And why?

In part because I have made it so with paint and plaster, bricks and stone and the sweat of my brow. Admittedly much of the gain came of crowding and competition for a place to live and breathe in the country, but there are also my twenty years at hard labor that have been put into it.

Wealth was made that way in days gone by. Most of it was made no other way. Economists talk of the days of the frontier, when a man could take a slice of worthless land and a wild wood patch and create a home and farm. John Webster built this house out of nothing, or next to nothing—out of unwanted field stone, sand from his own cellar, lime burned in local kilns and timber cut out of the woods. In some degree I follow his example to keep the house from falling on my head and to make it worth more than it was when I got it.

Do I hear a chuckle of ghostly merriment from the cellar? Perhaps Ben Yerkes had his troubles with the assessor and tax collector, levying tribute on the work of his hands.

VIII. My House Is Haunted

Somehow I should recover the grandfather's clock which once stood against the wall and left its outline there. It has ticked away a century, perhaps, and never changed its tune. In a clock's opinion the ancient laws of human living and working and thriving and losing do not change, but only rest awhile.

These more human ghosts are too insistent and exacting. They lay out more work than I have time to do. The ghost of a grandfather's clock is more comfortable company. The clock itself would be better.

IX

Hands Are for Handicrafts

His full name was John Frederick Van Horn, but we called him Van, of course. More affectionately he was "Old Van" in the twilight of his years. He was janitor in chief of the school buildings; political boss of Bryn Athyn on the side.

I believe there were no pickings in his political activities. But it was necessary that somebody should know which were the good Republicans on the primary ballot, and the community thirty years ago was willing to take Van's word for it. In his opinion there were no good Democrats on anybody's ticket. Nobody else knew much about it, and nobody cared much. Today we are all emphatically and sometimes bitterly opinionated in politics, but I suspect it has not made much difference in the kind of state and county government we get.

Van was much more than a brush-and-mop janitor. He was master of many handicrafts, and his kingdom was the cellar workshop of the main school building.

The scholarship which brought me from England to the United States covered board, lodging and tuition, but I was to work for pocket money and the maintenance and repair of my imported British wardrobe. Mostly I earned what was needed by working for Van and learned a lot by doing so.

Sweeping floors, washing windows, cleaning blackboards and beating the chalk from erasers were among my employments. So was winding up the gas machine. A truly rural gas service, in those days, was delivered to the door in steel cylinders, and pressure in the pipes was maintained by

IX. Hands Are for Handicrafts

an arrangement of heavy weights. I did not like winding up the gas machine and was grateful when pipes were laid to put the machine out of business. For this reason, perhaps, I have never shared the traditional American antipathy for public utilities, any more than I ever learned to like penny pretzels or sour pickles.

A bright spot among the week's chores was Saturday morning's assignment to clean and tidy the workshop. The morning's work also included the cashing of Van's pay check. There was no bank in the neighborhood, but Lafe Larue's blacksmith shop served some of a bank's purposes.

Lafe's was one of the last blacksmith shops to survive around Philadelphia, and the garage which now stands in its place does not make such good money. Lafe was a fine blacksmith, I believe, though I am no judge of horses' hooves and footwear. But my antique andirons and wood basket for the fireside are Lafe's handiwork. The andirons are built of horseshoes,

My Own Four Walls

bar iron and a Ford axle, and you could drop a cord of wood on them without cracking them.

On Saturday mornings I would present Van's check to the paying teller in the pleasing murk of the blacksmith's shop. I could wait sometimes while Lafe hugged a horse's fetlock and hammered on a shoe. Then without a word he would wipe his hands on a dirty apron, fish in his pocket and peel the money from a wad of bills the size of a fist. I remember that Van's weekly wage check never made any noticeable impression on its bulk. Several times Lafe was held up for his money and killed one thief with a baseball bat who tried to take it from him.

It was messing about among the tools on Saturday mornings that gave me the idea of learning to use them. I had tried a little "manual training" in an English board school at the age of ten or twelve, but nothing came of it except a footstool which could never keep all four feet on the ground at once. My only other experience with tools was in perpetually mending a secondhand bicycle and in the ancient and honorable hobby of fretwork. I had made overmantels, magazine racks, clockcases and even bookcases by fretwork, which is not the best way to build a bookcase. I found that in this misguided country a fret saw is called a jig saw and fretwork regarded as a merely childish amusement.

But Van's tools were real tools, and Van was not unwilling that I should use them. There is still a chest around the house that was put together in his workshop. It is of grained cypress, the lid of two pieces neatly mortised together. To be belatedly honest about it, I didn't mortise them. Even then I knew that a good carpenter suffers while he watches a bad one spoiling lumber. And I knew, too, that a little innocent admiration went a long way with Old Van. So Van showed me how to put two pieces of wood together by mortise and tenon, mainly by doing it himself.

The job was well finished with elbow grease, stain and wax, and one Saturday a crowd came in to see it. The reason turned out to be that one of the girls had spread word around that the Britisher was in the basement, "painting his chest."

Van was a good teacher in the patience and precision that carpentry calls for. A teacher in matters of more consequence was Jake Freeman, senior member of the janitorial staff.

IX. Hands Are for Handicrafts

It used to be said that there were two gentlemen in Bryn Athyn. One was a bishop by profession, a veteran of distinguished service in the Southern cause during the Civil War. The other was Jake Freeman, black as the coal stove and born a slave. We were good friends, and Jake was my boss in the province of sweeping and mopping.

I made a feeble job of cleaning the gymnasium one day and Van frowned on it. My excuses implied that somebody else was responsible, which could only be Jake Freeman or his assistant, Jimmy Morgan. Later I found Jake doing the job a second time. In sorrow, not anger, he reproved me.

"Sweep it bad if you wants, but don' let another man git the blame fer it. That ain't honest. I'm sweepin' it agin fer you, and it's wrong you should let 'm think I done it in the fust place. But I ain't saying nuthin.' I'm just sweepin' it agin."

My present sins of omission and commission will fill a book on judgment day, but since Jake Freeman taught me better I have tried not to shift the blame for bad sweeping onto somebody else.

In course of time I was promoted from the broom, bucket and blackboard to more exciting duties in plumbing and electrical repairs. Repairing the electrical equipment of those days was mainly a matter of inventing it all over again in order to find out what was the matter. After that you mended it, if possible. Unforeseen consequences of these educational investigations was that years later, during a schoolteacher's long summer vacations, I made a sort of living by wiring a dozen or more houses. Only one of them, I think, has burned down since then.

Plumbing was more of a man's game and Willy Van Horn, son of Old Van, my mentor in it. He taught me to cut a thread on a pipe and the curiously anatomical jargon of the plumbing profession, all joints and elbows and threads of both genders. But he would not teach me how to wipe a joint. Wiping a joint with melted lead was something reserved for the master's hand. I suppose it takes years and years to learn how to wipe a joint. I doubt it's worth it, either.

Plumbing is an interesting profession, but a little knowledge of it is a dangerous thing. When a pipe breaks in midwinter you may get the misguided idea that you can fix it. More likely the kitchen spigots will develop a drip and you will be elected or appointed to put in a new washer.

My Own Four Walls

This will be about seven o'clock in the evening, when you think you have better things to do. But the monotonous thumping in the sink has been driving the household crazy all day and will do the same to you in the middle of the night if you don't fix it. In the silent watches of the night a leaking spigot shatters the nerves like drumfire.

You could easily fix it, perhaps, if you could find anything remotely resembling a washer around the house or workshop. It turns out, too, that all washer stores for ten miles around are closed for the night and the local drugstore, taproom and moving-picture theater don't sell washers.

But let it be assumed that you have obtained a box of washers, red ones and white ones, of sundry sizes for all sorts of leaking spigots. You descend to the cellar to turn off the water. Comes a shout from the kitchen that the gas has gone out. You turn it on again and try elsewhere. Nothing seems to happen. You will discover later that you have disconnected the third-floor bathroom. You will also learn that somebody decided to wash out a pair of stockings while the water was shut off, gave up the idea for lack of water and left the spigot turned on. The evidence by that time will be seeping through the ceiling.

You finally choke off the leaking kitchen spigot by turning off everything in the cellar. The gas goes out, the oil burner stops running, howls of anguish come from the second-floor bathroom. You return grimly to the kitchen, tear apart the plumbing with a monkey wrench and look for the worn-out washer.

Well, there's the washer, all right! It's down inside the spigot and determined to stay there. You fumble for it with fingers, pliers, buttonhooks and oyster forks. The washer sits tight and sneers at you.

You get it out finally with one of you wife's hairpins, if she wears hairpins. You insert the new washer, tighten up the plumbing, turn on the water. The spigot still leaks, somewhat worse than before. You put a bucket under it and leave word with the family next morning that somebody can call a plumber.

An episode of my early education in handicrafts was a summer spent in supporting myself, while school was out, as carpenter's handy man on the building of a new school in the neighborhood. There were two of us, and Loyal Odhner was the other, and two more unpromising apprentices never toiled in the building trade. I don't think our heart was in our work.

IX. Hands Are for Handicrafts

One reason may be that our wages were $1.50 a day. Two others were Big Ed and Little Jack, also enlisted as carpenter's laborers.

Ed was big, bellicose and blasphemous. Jack was a poor creature but kindlier toward two schoolboys earning pocket money. He gave us well-meaning advice on not straining ourselves over heavy timbers, though Big Ed delighted to make us carry them. Both were experts in the art of making a little work go a long way. Both were bums, in fact, and could imagine no reason why we should consider ourselves anything better.

The job could not be called profitable, but its byproducts were a compensation when payday came round. For it soon occurred to us that building was not an esoteric art but mainly a matter of putting boards together with nails. Odds and ends of lumber were everywhere around the job, evidently a useless nuisance to the builders. There were also nails.

So when we were gently but firmly fired from our gainful employment our plans were already laid for the remainder of the summer. In the secrecy of a hospitable cellar we built ourselves a tree house from the gleanings of our daily labors. I was architect of the job and Loyal did the bullwork. The house was designed in portable pieces, the first sectional home ever constructed in the neighborhood, because we intended to erect it in a tract of private woods whose owner might not want a tree house there. On a Sunday morning, immediately after the church doors closed, we went to work at furious pace and hoisted the tree house thirty feet above ground in the embrace of four fine chestnut trees. For five years afterwards we slept there all summer long and sometimes in winter.

In building the tree house we barely finished the heavy hammering before church was out. The reason was that I had planned the roof in two pieces without anticipating that the overhanging eaves would be in the way of the trees or vice versa. So it was necessary to bite two holes out of the roof to let the trees through.

This soured me some on sectional houses, and I still don't like them. It is my old-fashioned conviction that houses should be built, not put together like jigsaw puzzles. And though in theory it may be a fine idea that a house should be shipped from factory to consumer in packages wrapped in cellophane, my experience is that the pieces don't fit.

It was a sectional garage that taught this lesson. Its specifications resembled those of the one-man top of early automobiles, which could sometimes be set up in a sudden rainstorm by two able-bodied passengers, a boy and a bystander. Makers of the garage likewise claimed that one handy man could throw it together in half a day.

Perhaps we picked the wrong day for it. George Heaton and I got the frame together somehow by stretching and sawing, then tried to lift the roof pieces into place. A high wind was blowing, and the roof sections developed the lift of an airplane wing and tried to fly away with us. When we got the roof down we found it three inches short in one direction, two inches long in the other. This was remedied somehow, and later the roof sagged in the middle and sat down on top of the car.

It was also one of the ugliest garages ever devised by the misguided mind of a man, even though all cut-price suburban garages are ugly as sin.

It was during the Freeland Kendrick administration of Philadelphia's affairs that I was invited to write a motion-picture scenario of the city's social, civic and industrial progress. Loyal was mixed up in the matter, and the two of us were guided all over the city to collect material for our story. Charlie Grakelow, then Director of Public Welfare, personally escorted us on a tour of his department, including Philadelphia's homes for the aged and unfortunate, its child clinics and playgrounds. Also we visited the House of Correction, where drunks and dopes and other undesirables are incarcerated to teach them better manners.

We arrived at the hour of evening inspection, the shabby inmates lined up. Second in line was Little Jack. Recognition was mutual. We shook hands, both feeling fairly uncomfortable. The Director of Public Welfare may have been astonished, except that nothing surprises an experienced director of public welfare.

It was by these youthful employments and experiences, in part, that I learned how to hit a nail on the head without knocking my thumb loose from its socket. Though it is not the ability to whack at a nail without bending it into a hairpin, or missing it altogether, that sets the carpenter apart from his clumsy fellows.

The test is how and where he holds the hammer. If he clutches it by the neck or at the waistline, he is a mere fumbler and amateur in the craft. But if he can swing the hammer freely, heftily and confidently from the handle's end and hit what he aims at squarely on the nose, he can begin to call himself a carpenter and none can say him nay.

X

Curing the Smoking Habit

Among the first parts of the house to challenge the spirit of reconstruction were its several fireplaces. All these were boarded up when we bought the place, and a couple or more were hidden by wallpaper. Holes in walls and ceilings showed that recent inhabitants preferred the comfort of potbellied coal and chunk stoves to the one-sided warmth of an open fire.

We found one fireplace in the living room, a friendly thing beneath a paneled mantel. There was another in the best bedroom, just wide and deep enough to warm a half a dozen small children while struggling through their morning exercises with buttons, strings and side garters. There was one in the cellar, which has never proved much help to light housekeeping. There is yet another, we suspect, behind the wall in the second bedroom, but we shall leave it there or leave the matter in doubt until our old age is in need of adventure. Anyone who exhausts all the surprises of life at once has none but himself to blame for boredom.

In addition to these there was the grandfather of all fireplaces in what had been formerly the farmhouse kitchen. A cavernous affair, four feet deep and six feet wide, and lofty enough so that one might stand inside and look up to a distant square of daylight.

Its plastered face was supported by a great timber, probably oak, black with age and smoke and with the marks of the ax still on it. In the back of the fireplace was a brick oven built into the wall, with iron door and no outlet otherwise. We puzzled about it, in our civilized ignorance, not

knowing how cooking could be done in such an oven, until some old-timer told us that a wood fire should be built inside the oven, its embers taken out and the meat inserted to roast in the heat of the bricks about it.

On one of our first festive occasions in the house we recklessly resolved to use the oven. Ducks were to be the *pièce de résistance* of the meal. Every cookbook has recipes for cooking ducks, but none of them mentions a brick oven in the back of a kitchen fireplace.

Do you, perchance, have a fireless cooker in your cellar which you will never use again? Most households do. Most housewives, at one time or other, fell for the idea that fuel could be saved and food better cooked by putting it into hot storage for an hour or two. And at that time it was thought to be the last word in culinary matters.

It was the accepted way of cooking a century or more ago. And it still worked with the ducks, though the cook nearly collapsed from nervous

X. Curing the Smoking Habit

strain while waiting to open the oven door. The ducks might be raw, the ducks might be burned to cinders.

The ducks were done to a turn, the ducks were delicious. But once was enough, and all ducks since then have been done in a gas stove.

The fireplace itself, aside from the brick oven, was big enough to cook a cow in. But we had no cow, and the only remaining purpose for the fireplace was for a fire on a frosty autumn evening when lighting the furnace seemed a little premature and a lot of trouble too.

Almost at once we discovered that the fireplace smoked. It smoked so much that we threw water on the fire and fled to the living room. It smoked over anything short of a fire that might have burned the house down. I could have wept over that fireplace. And if you had sat there, with a log burning brightly on the hearth and smoke billowing forth at every breath of breeze above the chimney, you would have wept too.

So I announced with certainty that I would fix that chimney when warmer weather came and discovered then that it was full of birds' nests. This seemed to explain everything, so I worried no more about it until early winter. And with the first frosty evening I found that the fireplace still smoked.

I noticed at once that the chimney was too low for the rest of the house and that to raise it a few feet would be pleasant employment for a summer vacation. I raised it by four feet the following summer and by five more in the succeeding spring. The fireplace still smoked, a little more viciously, if possible, than before.

After a long cold winter of meditation I decided that the chimney should be hooded, or capped, and when summer came I crowned it with a slab of slate, leaving four outlets for the smoke from the fireplace. When winter came again I found out that the smoke never got far enough up the chimney to discover the outlets and that in the meantime the wind blew into them from all quarters of the compass and spouted smoke all over the dining room. Furthermore, there came a storm which blew against my slab of slate, and it fell off and down through the roof. So at last I called into conference all the local contractors, builders, architects, civil engineers and uncivil plumbers.

They came and looked solemnly at my fireplace and sat around it and stood inside it and peered up the chimney and measured the hearth and

My Own Four Walls

made sketches. Several suggested that they would fix the fireplace forever for $75. So I decided, once again, to fix it myself.

I fixed it for several summers in succession by raising the hearth and building the opening smaller and bricking up the oven and inserting a smoke shelf and a damper. It still smoked, as it must have smoked since its dead-and-gone builder of the early nineteenth century gathered field stones from his farm and thought he was making a fireplace. Sometimes it smoked more, sometimes less, but always it smoked. At intervals I put it to prolonged tests and sat in front of its fuming face until I was cooked and smoked to the consistency of a kipper or a picnic ham, considering and rejecting a thousand remedies for its obstinacy. It still smoked.

So at last I turned to Washington, whence all blessings flow. I sent for all available bulletins on the construction and care of fireplaces and some others on beekeeping and concrete construction for pigpens, which are also among the concerns of our national government. When the pamphlets came, with the compliments of the Department of Agriculture, I read them all through and compared them critically with my fireplace. It seemed that none of them had ever heard of such a fireplace.

So finally I threw them into the fireplace, which immediately smoked its head off.

So I nearly gave up the battle. I installed another hot-water radiator and learned to change the subject when visitors admired the fireplace and wondered why there should be no fire in it. The fireplace had smoked for a century; it would probably smoke another unless I cured it completely by refraining from lighting a fire in it.

But one day there came a handy man to the door, looking for work. I needed no handy man, but he needed a job and Christmas was coming, when I would like to lay a Yule log on the fire and make merry over it. In an inspired and unreasoning moment I took him to my fireplace and told him its troubles. He nodded his head wisely and asked for three buckets of sand, some cement and a hatful of bricks.

These I gave him, and for a day or so he poked around within my fireplace, smearing its inward parts, arching its back and shaping its sides, covering the nakedness of its ancient masonry and entirely obliterating its oven. He used no blueprints or government bulletins, nor any rule or

X. Curing the Smoking Habit

plumb. But when the work was done and dry we lit a fire in that ancient fireplace and it flared straight up the chimney.

There was no science in this miracle, nor can I tell its secret. It must have been a genius that came to my door and went away well satisfied with his work and its recompense. Or it may have been Santa Claus himself, taking holiday before his busy season. I still do not know how to cure the smoking habit in a wrongly built chimney. I doubt anybody knows much about it, though modern builders and architects know how to build a chimney better than John Webster built this one.

Yet the comforting fire that crackles on my hearth, whenever I can find logs to burn or the kids have cracked up another dining-room chair, may prove a point of some importance. The man who made the chimney draw was using no blueprint skills but his American birthright of handiness with tools. I do not much doubt that he could build himself a whole house by the same instinct and experience, if you would give him time.

As the house was enlarged with wings—though they look more like fins—it was decided to shift the dining room somewhere else, and the old kitchen was given the title of the study or sometimes the library. If I ever have sufficient time, peace and quiet for studying, I have a fine place for it. The room is oddly shaped with a peaked ceiling and crooked corners. The stonework of the fireplace staggers up like steps of a Mexican pyramid, leaving dark and cobwebby corners between wall and chimney. During the prohibition period I stored my home-brew there until one night a gallon jug of hard cider blew up and spilled itself all over twenty-four volumes of the world's best literature.

It is a room in which to dream and see visions. It is a room for long and enlightening conversation, as when Henry Tetlow dropped in one evening for light refreshments and was still there when the dawn came up like thunder over the blackberry patch.

I suppose a properly planned house should have a conversation room, no less than a laundry and library. But even then there might be lacking sufficient opportunities for friends to talk at length on matters that are worth the trouble. Civilization seems to be in some sort of conspiracy against this humane and harmless practice. There is no place for it, no time for it, no patience for it in a world that is hurrying hotfoot to nowhere.

If it were not for business and bridge and golf and gardening and

My Own Four Walls

reading and radio and airplanes and automobiles, a man might now and then find time and place to talk a topic to a sufficient finish with a friend and equal, for no useful purpose except the pure pleasure of good-tempered argument. But, as Henry Tetlow has often said, the grave fault of the modern world in general and the United States in particular is that there is no place to sit down.

Someday the study will be formally dedicated as a place to sit down. Right now the younger generation gets most use of it, whether for throwing darts, practicing on the snare drum or toasting marshmallows by the fire. But someday I shall reclaim my own.

A man of letters should have a study in his house, though it was Henry Tetlow, once again, who recalled "the pitiable plight of Agamemnon Peterkin, who, having completed vast preparations, sat down in the circle of his admiring family to write a book—and then could think of nothing to write about." The study's setup for literary endeavor is perfect. There are great books on its high shelf, picked up at country sales or at Leary's famous secondhand store, and I might live fifty years longer and never look in one of them. There is a Blake engraving of The Canterbury Pilgrims above the fireplace. There are old bean pots and a Toby jug.

But the truth of it is that I can write more and better in a cluttered office downtown, sitting on a familiar chair at a familiar typewriter and staring sometimes out the window of the Ledger Building at the tower of Independence Hall. When the wheels stop turning and there is a large blank area where my brain ought to be I lean on that tower until something turns up.

The study will serve its purpose better, maybe, when there are not so many domestic distractions to disturb its peace and quiet. And it may also be mentioned that one of the penalties of a journalistic career is that no writer's wife ever takes him seriously. She may love him within reason, rejoice in his reputation and defend his fair name against the slings and arrows of the neighbors, who are invariably of the opinion that no writing man can be quite respectable. But she never believes, in her heart, that he has anything important to do.

I have great admiration for wives, both in general and particular. They are efficient in their fields and have made a much better job of their personal evolution than most of their masculine associates. They can and do

X. Curing the Smoking Habit

get through an appalling amount of obligations every working day and top off the week with a Sunday that carries requirements of cleaner faces and clothing for children, the persuasion of a husband to church and preparation of a monumental Sabbath dinner.

How they do it no man knows, not even myself, who have served my apprenticeship with the dishpan and eke the mop. I can wash dishes and have done so, but it ruins the day for me and most of the following week, not to mention the dishes. It is too complicated a job; it exhausts a man. But a wife tosses it off without a thought.

In other words, wives are so efficient within their province that I am willing to leave it to them. I would fain do so, certainly, while in the agonies of communion with the Muses, who are the most trifling, flighty, unmanageable, unmannerly and unresponsive hussies that a man can serve or woo. When I sit in the trance of a yogi, with a vacant stare in my eye and my mouth open, I may not seem to be at work or even thinking. But I am certainly fit for nothing else.

There are obscure passages in Shakespeare where one may reverently suspect that he forgets what he is talking about. Might it be that these dusky patches mark the moments when sweet Anne called on him to peel potatoes? Homer is said to nod now and then. Can it be that he was called from his verses to interview the huckster? Pope writes bad lines here and there and perhaps everywhere. Maybe he often lost a couplet in an epithet when his landlady insisted that he carry coal to the kitchen stove.

One other objection to the study is that its fireplace has a frightful appetite for wood. And wood, in the modern world, has become expensive stuff. It takes some of the edge from a festive evening by the fireside to reflect that you are throwing fuel on the fire of friendship at the rate of $16 a cord.

XI

Cobwebs on the Classics

It is on my mind that the farmhouse kitchen, some of these days, shall become the sanctuary for culture and conversation that it ought to be. It goes now by the name of the library, but I might almost as well refer to the outside kitchen as the scullery. It is the library because there are a great many books in it, but I wait for a more leisurely existence in which to read them.

It sometimes concerns my conscience that I shall never read them. Many of them are excellent books to own, but the sort which you postpone reading until a rainy day. But when the rainy day arrives the youngsters are throwing darts or playing drums in the library, and I don't read them.

A few minutes of browsing in a man's library may tell more about him than his diary, bank account or tombstone. My own books would betray me, to somebody who didn't know any better, as a confirmed classicist and lover of fine bindings, with a special weakness for Latin and the novels of Sir Walter Scott.

This may be due, in part, to the fashion in which I set about furnishing a roomful of books some sixteen years ago. About that time we enlarged the house a little, so that the old kitchen, which had served six years as a dining room, was set free for other uses. And about that time, too, I lost my job as schoolteacher and went to clerking in the city, with a full hour free for lunch and not much money to spare for the lunch

Three blocks away was Leary's Old Bookstore, a landmark in literature for a century.

Charming books have been written about the amenities of book

XI. Cobwebs on the Classics

collecting and the insidious lure of first editions. Equipped with sound judgment, literary knowledge and more money than he knows what to do with, a man may find great fun in collecting Kiplings and Cabells, letters of Lincoln and state papers of Washington, old school primers and the works of Pastor Weems. But this kind of stuff costs money.

There is another sort of book collecting that will hardly strain the leanest purse. That is to seek, find and purchase a book for ten cents at Leary's.

Other cities than Philadelphia have their wayside inns for books of passage, purgatories of paper and print, potter's fields for many books which nobody will give decent burial. But Leary's is little less than a national institution, a secondhand bookstore of magnificent dimensions. And among its attractions in those days was a five-tier, fifty-foot shelf devoted entirely to books priced at ten cents.

That was in summertime, and it seems that in summer people either sell more books or buy less. So in hot weather the store erupted its surplus onto the outside shelf. Books that had enjoyed false security and fancy prices were sold for a dime to pay for their overdue lodging. The outside shelf was the last judgment on literature and the melting pot of the brains of men. And I suppose that a book which would not sell for ten cents went to the mill to be boiled down again and made into paper towels.

I spent thirty minutes a day and a dime a time, during that summer, picking up a library from the ten-cent shelf. Most of the books were venerable, used and worn, as is most of the world's wisdom. Doubtless they were full of germs, but so were their authors. The great majority of them were overpriced, even at ten cents, but the great majority I did not buy. It was the remnant and residue that I sought after, and if I found one small pearl in so many bivalves I considered a dime well spent.

A certain conscience should be developed for the buying of books, even ten-centers, or else a library becomes a confusion of tongues. It might be wise to buy no book treating of matters outside the conceivable domain of interest, even though its binding matches the library furniture. A ten-cent shelf has books on basket weaving, dentistry and aboriginal ceramics, but somebody else may buy them.

A second rule is that a book ought not to be bought because it matches a book you own already. For ten cents apiece I picked up half a

My Own Four Walls

dozen volumes of belles-lettres, part of a so-called "universal library," and am glad to own them. It was a temptation to take seven others, the Memoirs of Continental Courts, but at the time I could imagine no reason for owning a collection of continental memoirs. I can't think of any now, for that matter.

Thirdly, the book should be one that I might possibly, conceivably, eventually read. This does not mean that I have read or expect to read all my books. But as I have more ties than I can wear, as I own pipes that I shall never smoke again, as flowers grow in my garden that will never be plucked, smelled or noticed, so my library offers an opulence of choice and infinity of resource that have little respect to the small spare time a modern man gets for reading.

In the fourth place, no book should be forgiven for poor paper or bad print and hardly for bad binding. Books should be substantial and decent, though they cost but ten cents, and even this is not incompatible with the purchase price. Witness my five volumes of George Eliot, all dressed in good leather, which explains why they have lived to tell their tale again. Also a sound copy of Rasselas, surely an oversight of the presiding deity of the ten-cent shelf. Here are five fat volumes of Dickens containing thirteen of his novels, bound in leather and not in bad repair. Why so cheap? Because, forsooth, the set is incomplete. Yet thirteen tales from Dickens are probably plenty.

A single volume of Duruy's *History of Greece and Rome* might have been considered a poor day's catch. To collect five more was a triumph; to find four of them in sequence a benefaction of special Providence. And a copy of Scott's *Antiquary* started me fishing for more, and a week's search turned up twelve volumes in the same edition. Actually I read a lot of them but ran foul of *Peveril of the Peak* and gave up Sir Walter as a man who wrote too much about people who have been dead too long.

Thirty cents bought five inches of Dr Eliot's five-foot shelf, but the three books compass nearly all classic English poetry that is worth reading. From the same generous shelves I have three Shakespeares. One cannot have too many Shakespeares, which may be why I own another, in two volumes, so large that the only convenient way to carry it is in an express wagon. Add to these the plays of Euripides, the poems of Emerson, Marcus Aurelius, *Don Quixote*, *Sartor Resartus*, Xenophon on Socrates, Macaulay's

XI. Cobwebs on the Classics

History of England, six volumes of Gibbon's *Decline and Fall.* Who will grudge for any of these the price of a ham sandwich?

If a man can read he need not die ignorant. Twelve harmonious volumes of science have left the ten-cent shelf for a better home in my library. Here are Darwin's *Origin of Man,* Adam Smith's *Wealth of Nations,* Tyndall's essays, Hegel's *Philosophy of History,* Bacon's *Novum Organum,* Huxley's addresses and others as imposing. Have I read them? No. Have you?

Outside the classic lies a vast and fertile field. When you have nothing better to do you may borrow and read my ten-cent copy of *Is Mankind Advancing?*, which will probably confirm your suspicion that it isn't. Or spend ten cents' worth of time with Disraeli's *Curiosities of Literature.* Here, too, is plenty of poetry and collections of short stories and odd volumes of books in series or of some many-volumed work of history. But let it be admitted that there are many voluminous masterpieces of which one installment is sufficient.

The best memorials to human genius find their way eventually to the ten-cent shelves. The novels of today, the transient fads of philosophy or art, the technical treatises of trade live on the sheltered shelves and name their own price. But in the open air, begging for an owner, herded with the least among books, are the wise thoughts of the ancients and the classics of all literature.

There is a book in the library which may rate a special word. It is Darwin's *Origin of Species,* and I have owned it since I was seventeen. The first book I ever bought with my own money, and why I can't tell you.

That was when I worked in a British brewery, and among my reading was an English magazine known as *The Reader,* its price tuppence. *The Reader* ran a contest for amateur writers, calling for a 200-word essay on what the world would be like in the year 2000 or thereabouts. Unbeknownst to the old folks at home I wrote my story, sent it away and some weeks later woke up to find half the prize money, about $2.50, waiting on the door mat. That was a week's wages, and the family said I should spend it as I pleased. I bought a new violin bow, a necktie and Darwin's *Origin of Species.*

I was seventeen years old, and it was seventeen years later before I wooed the Muse again. She came through with $4.60 for a bit of verse,

My Own Four Walls

and I wonder still how editors figure such odd prices for the poetry they buy.

The Reader went out of business with the second issue after my essay was published. And shortly after he bought my verses the other editor died and so did his magazine. I wasn't much of a writer in those days, but I was sudden death to magazines and editors.

A considerable number of books on the library shelves refer back to the time when I held the high title of literary critic to *The Forum* magazine, which has also passed away. For more than a year I read everything that the publishers sent me, or nearly, and almost died of it.

As I recall that period of high literary pressure, I absorbed the publishers' output very much as the sea lions swallow their fish rations at the zoo. They went down whole and so quickly that they were nearly tasteless.

I am able to blush now for smacking with a wisecrack a book which somebody spent a year in writing and which I spent thirty minutes reading. Yet I also wonder how I could help it. I was supposed to read at least twenty books a month and browse around in others. I was required to read, mark and inwardly digest them, estimate their literary importance, evaluate their reader interest and moral influence, check their scholarship, criticize their style and dish up the results in trenchant phrase and pointed paragraph for an average fee of about $3.00 per book. Also I got the books, and a lot of them are still lying around.

It now seems significant that the best review written during my term of office came from a bed of pain in the Murray Hill Hospital, New York City, where Dr J. F. Montague spent ten days making me fit for another twenty years of living. I shall not discuss the operation, though the topic is tempting. But when I came out of it, a little low in spirits and lacking some nonessentials of my internal arrangements, I settled to the reading of a three-foot stack of books and dictated my etherized opinion of them to an obliging friend, Frank Townsend, sitting by the bedside with pencil and paper and some knowledge of shorthand.

When Edward C. Aswell, then acting editor of *The Forum*, received the result his enthusiasm knew no bounds, except that he somehow managed to refrain from raising my rate of compensation. He did suggest that the management should see to it that I had a monthly operation, not too serious, in advance of every book-section dead line.

XI. Cobwebs on the Classics

Subsequently I learned from Dr Montague that I came from the operating table with a pint or so of morphine in my system and was kept in a condition of mild anesthesia for a week thereafter. It was evident that I had written my masterpiece of book reviewing while *non compos mentis*.

In this circumstance there is something gravely significant. I would not go so far as to say that book critics should all be chloroformed for the general good of art and letters. It might be sufficient if they were merely drunk. But personal experience is proof that a readable and reasonably virulent review of thirty books may be written while under the influence of anesthetics. The same effect might be obtained, perhaps, by hitting the critic on the back of the head with a length of lead pipe or by spinning him rapidly in a cream separator.

An uninformed visitor might find it curious that my library contains vast quantities of schoolbooks on every conceivable educational topic. Some of these reflect the fact that in my pedagogic days I taught freshman Latin, English, geometry, Hebrew and almost anything else that no other and older member of the faculty wanted to teach. The most juvenile teacher on anybody's faculty gets the leavings. Since this includes the freshman class, an aggregation of adolescents who are neither fish, fowl nor good red herring and are consequently in need of special wisdom and guidance, it now appears to me that no teacher under forty years of age should be permitted to practice outside the college department.

But the glut of schoolbooks in my library is mainly due to the fact that every self-respecting teacher, during his summer vacation, plans to use a new textbook when the new term begins. Sometimes teacher has published his own textbook, a vast improvement on all previous textbooks on the same subject.

The result is that every autumn, for a dozen years past, some young member of the family has demanded money to buy a book of Caesar's *Gallic Wars*. In the library, probably, are twenty copies of Caesar's *Gallic Wars*, including a few interlinears confiscated in the days when I was teaching Latin. None of them will do. Teacher has selected a new and better high-school edition of Caesar's *Gallic Wars*, and the price is only a trifling $2.00. Similarly I am grievously overstocked with books on English composition, elementary algebra, geography, physics and chemistry.

My Own Four Walls

There are other Latin books which belong to my own pedagogical background. It is now incredible that I could ever read them, much less persuade small boys to read them. Here are Vergil, Cicero, Catullus, Ovid and Tacitus, some in swell leather editions. Over their shelf I should inscribe the most searching commentary ever made on classical studies, though I cannot recall who made it. "A gentleman need not know Latin, but he should, at least, have forgotten it."

A plethora of English poetry in the library is due to a former habit, or weakness, for attending country auction sales. At one of them were sold, "to the highest and best-approved bidder for cash," about twenty volumes of classic verses in bindings gay with gold leaf. The cobwebs that entwine the works of Cowper, Dryden, Hood and Lord Tennyson may prove that I prefer Edna St Vincent Millay and Dorothy Parker.

There is grave need for a good house cleaning in the library, where some shelves are doubled up with rows of books that nobody ever reads. But I have no heart for throwing books away or burning them. Admittedly I sold them by the suitcaseful in the days of book reviewing, but poverty must excuse it. Some good books got away by that route, and their loss is now repented.

It is hard to house-clean a bookshelf. It might be done by inaugurating a liberal loan policy in literature, since there is nothing less likely to return to its owner than a borrowed book. For a borrowed book is dangerously like a borrowed idea, which a man will adopt and use as his own without a trace of apology and at last believe that he invented it himself.

Yet it should be a social duty and pleasure to return a book to its owner, for he who carries home a book bears in his hand a good occasion for exchange of opinion and argument, for comparisons of taste and judgment, for all that inspires the pleasant art of conversation. You cannot discover such things in the return of an umbrella when it has stopped raining or the home-coming of the bridge tables and teaspoons when the party is over.

So the return of borrowed books might prove a stimulant to intelligent neighborliness. It might bring back some vagabond masterpieces to my own shelves. It might also get rid of three volumes of Balzac, a vegetarian cookbook and two novels by James Branch Cabell which accuse my conscience every time I come across them.

XII

What Am I Bid?

When my friends and neighbors start fixing over their houses and enlarging them, as many do when they recover from the financial strain of the second mortgage, I think gloomily of the furniture it will take to fill their bigger living rooms, extra bedrooms and sun porches. Such essential accessories to civilized living as tables and chairs, beds and bureaus, do not appear in the architect's blueprints. But a house is a poor thing without them.

We found that out when we moved into our farmhouse in the late summer of 1918. The furniture that had served well enough for two rooms and part share in a laundry tub was not enough for seven rooms and a bath. And by that time the architects and contractors had all our money and the Churchville Building and Loan Association, with monotonous regularity, was nicking the budget for $35 a month.

The solution was the country sale, at that time a recognized and respected feature of truly rural life. It has almost disappeared since then in the odor of gasoline. But it furnished our house, nearly a quarter century ago, at a cost that now seems incredible if not ridiculous.

I went to my first country sale by accident, my second by design and after that by a kind of habit and craving. Mention of an auction sale within navigable distance became like a whiff of whisky to a dipsomaniac. By hook or crook I would be there, bidding my head off for chairs and china, bureaus and boxbushes, gallon jugs and garden tools.

In cold truth I confess that I once bid on a bowling alley near Fox Chase, a thousand-gallon storage tank at Somerton, a ton of secondhand bricks in Southampton. Happily I didn't get them at my price. But I did buy a pump for fifty cents, though my farmhouse well was out of business.

My Own Four Walls

And I bid sixty cents for a live pig at Trevose, mainly to make conversation, and found I owned the wretched animal. Fortunately a farmer wanted my bargain more than I did and took it off my hands.

The trouble in those days was that I could spend a pleasant afternoon and $3.50 at a country sale and come home with a wagonload of apparently desirable plunder. It did not look so desirable when unloaded on the porch and surveyed by a critical wifely eye.

So sometimes I would swear off of country sales. But the day would inevitably come when I would slip away unostentatiously, edge my way into the crowd and fall again under the auctioneer's spell.

The auctioneer was usually Squire Ely, of Huntingdon Valley, who became accustomed to my presence at his elbow and would hardly start the sale until I showed up. I think now that he took advantage of my innocence and eager appetite for a bargain. When nobody else would buy a faded frying pan, an egg beater and a pepper grinder I usually found myself owning the aggregation for a knockdown price of five cents.

But it wasn't all junk that I bought at the country sales of Montgomery and Bucks counties. I know now that for a period my house was strewn with trophies of profound historical interest and some commercial value. The most comfortable chairs I ever owned once graced the barroom of the Lady Washington Inn, and everybody of any importance in our neighborhood had sat in them. I think I paid fifty cents apiece for them.

I paid precisely ten cents for a vast four-poster bed. I believe it was made of cherry wood, and it had never known a spring or mattress. Their early American equivalent was a lattice of rope attached to pegs, probably intended to be surmounted by an over-all pillow of goose feathers.

Ten cents was not much for a bed, but in those days beds were difficult to sell at auction. You could never be sure what else you might get with the bed. So for a dime I bought a bed so big that I had to cut four inches from its posts before it would stand in the "master's bedroom." By some perspiring ingenuity I substituted a spring for its network of roping, and for years it was a good enough bed for all practical purposes.

Then we got tired of it. It was the mischief to move for cleaning, and not even our best friends would tell us its true ancestry and value. So I sawed it up one day for firewood.

Not long later I was in the Lee Mansion in Arlington, Va. There, in

XII. What Am I Bid?

solemn state, stood my ten-cent bed. The uniformed gentleman on duty assured me that it was an almost unique specimen of early American furniture. I did not tell him that I had burned one like it in the living-room fireplace.

In the Lee Mansion, somewhere in the servants' quarters, I also came upon a charming child's coach with high wheels behind and little ones before. I bought the same coach for $1.50 at a country auction sale in Bucks County.

I cannot imagine why the ingenuity of modern baby-coach manufacturers ignores the genius of our early American ancestors. They knew a great deal, and they certainly knew how to build baby coaches.

That coach carried our first three youngsters on their earliest adventures. It would ride easily through high grass, over rough roads, uphill and downdale. You could push it anywhere, with a large child in the upper seat and a smaller one in the lower. So it was worn out at last, and I never knew I had been shoving around a valuable antique until I found its twin at Arlington.

The baby coach was an afterthought to one of my most reckless afternoons. The sale was held some miles away, but I got there somehow, with the understanding that young Camille Vinet would call for me and my purchases at late afternoon. Cammy was a pupil in one of my classes. The idea was that I should teach him Latin. It was a thoroughly silly idea.

Cammy was the son of Professor Vinet, himself a true classical scholar, but the gift for Latin and Greek is not hereditary. Young Camille had none of it. Yet it did not matter much, for the son emerged from his Latin studies, which were totally unsuccessful, to become the personal airplane pilot and confidante of Governor George H. Earle, of Pennsylvania, and a man of some substance in the Commonwealth's political affairs.

But at that time Cammy was an unhappy Latin student and the personal friend and manager of Napoleon, Professor Vinet's angular and discouraged horse. I believe that Napoleon has since passed way, and it would be a miracle if he hadn't. I have never met a horse that could play dead so convincingly in the prime of life. Cammy showed up at the sale with Napoleon and the wagon, but the sale was by no means over and Cammy could not stay. So he left the wagon and Napoleon and went back to his father's farm to finish his chores.

My Own Four Walls

When the sale was over I had purchased a small mountain of stuff, including the baby coach. Napoleon looked at the heap and seemed to sag in the middle. I had unhappy visions of driving a dead horse along the byways of Bucks County.

So I loaded a fair proportion of the purchases on the wagon, the rest on the baby coach. Down the by-lanes and along County Line Road I led the horse with one hand, pushed the coach with the other. Napoleon homeward plodded his weary way, eying every ditch as a possible place to lie down and die. No horse ever traveled slower without stopping entirely.

Halfway home we met Cammy, his day's work done and looking for Napoleon. Without comment he put the baby coach and its contents on the wagon, invited me to sit by the driver and whaled Napoleon expertly on the rear elevation. Napoleon pricked up his ears, kicked up his heels and galloped all the way home.

XII. What Am I Bid?

In those days there was usually a dim background of tragedy to the comedy of the country sale. Somebody had died and ancient treasures had no longer a guardian. The farm was a failure and the family on its way to safer city living. The sheriff had laid unwilling hands on a neighbor's property to satisfy a careless debt.

So the house was naked and ashamed and the garden returning to chaos under careless feet. Neighbors would be there, avidly and politely curious as at an interesting funeral. Some strangers, too, with an appraising eye for spoil, and junk dealers like birds of prey around the remains.

Squire Ely was a commanding personality with a miraculous capacity for continuous oration and an instantaneous eye for the half-formed bid. He wove a spell. Useless articles became eminently desirable as he discussed them. He had a sort of humor, mainly expressed in pleasantries concerning bedroom china and rolling pins. Nor would he tolerate an undisciplined spirit in the audience. If you would not take a forced bargain for five cents, you could bid in vain for a better one.

The country sale, in those days, began with small farm and garden tools. A good spade would go for fifteen cents, but after that the squire would sell three barn forks for twice their worth. Odds and ends of old iron would drop at the feet of the junk dealers, a curious crew, dirty of skin and flavored with gin. They would buy anything and hoped to sell everything and had more money in the bank than most of us.

Back of the house would be lined up the farm machinery. It was easy to buy an obsolete plow or harrow for twenty-five cents. You got a lot for your money, but you didn't have anything. And if a man owned a horse for which he had no particular respect or regard, he could equip him here completely if not elegantly.

Next came the cattle and horses, the phlegmatic pigs and scared sheep. This was the most picturesque point of the afternoon. It is very pleasant to sit on a barn wall in October sunshine with the affectionate smells of a farmyard drifting around you and watch a pageant of patient cows and horses, prodded forth from the barn to listen without protest to an eloquent glorification of their past and future.

The cow, perhaps, is lean and angular and notably jaded by her long journey along the milky way, but the auctioneer considers her the only and original cow. He gets no more than $20 for her, which does not surprise

My Own Four Walls

him much. Horses are galloped to and fro by energetic assistants who try to inspire their steeds with their own enthusiasm. But when they come to rest under the auctioneer's hammer they are sold for small money.

Back of the house the farmers' wives are rocking rhythmically in a variety of chairs, awaiting their opportunity. The auctioneer gets around to the furniture with a new audience and a fresh zest. He displays sleight of hand; a broken chair becomes miraculously whole as he talks about it. By more magic ten-cent-store stuff becomes rare china and cut glass and brings more than its worth. There is brisk bidding for washtubs, carpet sweepers and plush furniture stuffed within an inch of its life.

Visiting gentlewomen who have come in big cars in quest of antiques have their turn when an old cradle is held up for bids. Heaven knows how they can possibly need a cradle, but they want very badly the baby's bed which some Pennsylvania farmer fashioned out of plain wood by a pattern that goes far back, perhaps to the days when Ben Yerkes bought my house and decided to raise a family in it.

Before the antique hounds became too plentiful we bought that kind of cradle at a country sale. Outstanding advantage of that sort of cradle is that when the baby falls out of bed, as babies do, he has not far to fall. They were hooded against drafts and could be rocked by the kick of a foot, and I hope the baby liked it.

Half a dozen of ours set out on the voyage of life in such a cradle, picked up at a country sale for ninety cents. But if you want one now, you must go to an antique dealer and pay $20 for it. I might, under skillful persuasion, take less for mine.

But in those days the mystic alchemy of the word "antique" had not reached our neck of the woods. I was once mystified, admittedly, when a professional in the game paid $9.00 for a pair of Dolphin candlesticks. But before that I had bought a five-rung ladder-back chair for fifty cents, and the kids thought it lots of fun and kicked it to pieces in six weeks.

At one such sale I bought, among other things, a good Willcox and Gibbs sewing machine for $2.50 and a suite of dining-room furniture for $6.00. There was snow on the ground, and the roads and farm lanes were deep with mud. By no means could I get my purchases out of there. But the farmer said they could stay in his barn all winter, and so they did. When the spring sun dried the roads I called for them and found them all there.

XII. What Am I Bid?

At the same sale, somewhere in Bucks County, I took a fifty-cent chance on an assortment of gallon jugs and crocks lying beside a farmyard fence. Among the rubbish was a curious bottle of pale yellow glass with a wheat-sheaf pattern on its side. It looked like a poor kind of bottle to me and I put it away in the cellar.

Some years later a wealthy friend proudly showed his collection of early American glassware. Among the exhibits was the duplicate of my bottle. Under questioning he admitted paying $7.50 for it, probably too much. I gave him my bottle. One fragment of early American glassware, after all, does not make a collection.

But twenty years ago or more the fictitious values of the collector had not yet ruined the country sale. You paid what you thought the thing was worth in service to your own household. You bought a lot of junk, because houses in those days were crowded with junk. Probably they still are.

The twilight of a truly rural auction sale, in those days, was a touching scene.

It is getting late. The auctioneer is not hoarse but he is thirsty. Folks are going home. So the last of the furniture is suddenly knocked down for next to nothing, which is why I once bought a set of bird's-eye maple furniture for $6.00 and found the top drawer of the bureau, locked and the key lost, packed tight with good towels and sheets and old linen.

Wagons disappear down the road with furniture sticking out all over them. Ford cars of aboriginal vintage groan more than usual under heavy loads. The auctioneer and clerk check their sheets and count their money. It is all there. For some reason those who attended these country sales were innocently honest.

The house is bare, the garden wrecked and dotted with useless purchases which men are afraid to take home to their apprehensive wives. A lone figure perches atop a shapeless pile of furniture, scrapple pans, picture frames, fence posts and chicken wire, waiting for Napoleon to come and carry it home.

That must be me.

XIII

Why Wives Leave Home

Climax of the country sale period, a paroxysm of petty extravagance which almost cured me, was the two-day auction which disposed of the personal and household effects of an elderly lady named Barnsley, a resident of Bethayres, Pa. I never met her but believe she had lived long alone and was locally considered a little queer. The stuff she left behind her seemed to say so.

In one locked closet of her house were found forty hats. All over the place were trinkets of china, especially coffee cups. There were great quantities of yard goods, probably picked up in bargain basements. For a dozen years since then the difficulty of dressing small children for Halloween and other costume parties has been met by digging among the fabrics bought at the Barnsley sale.

Crisis of the sale was when the auctioneer opened a bedroom door and found its floor a foot deep in odds and ends of every imaginable character. A bomb dropped in a ten-cent store might create the same kind of chaos. Not even Squire Ely, who would auction off a secondhand mousetrap as willingly as a suite of horsehair furniture, could face the problem of sorting and selling what lay before him. He announced that the total contents of the room, whatever they might be, would be sold in one piece to the highest bidder.

There is a gambling spirit within me which rarely gets much exercise. When it does it costs me more than it is worth. But in the heady excitement of the Barnsley sale I would have taken a chance on anything. Two others, Fred Finkeldey and Loyal Odhner, were willing to pool resources with me to buy the room. The final price was $40.

Getting the stuff away when the sale was over loaded a big touring

XIII. Why Wives Leave Home

car twice. We spread it on three long tables and the women went to work on it, taking turns at making their choice. It took two long evenings to go through it, and what was left went into bushel baskets for the trash collector.

Madame Barnsley, whether maid, wife or widow, must have been a curious character with a strange taste in collecting. There were three dozen necklaces on the floor, few of much value. There were dozens of small pieces of jade jewelry, some worth substantial money. There were fourteen new toothbrushes, several pairs of masculine suspenders and some men's belts brittle with age. There were women's hats covering several decades of rural fashion and fragments of false teeth. There were souvenir shaving mugs, shoebrushes, several dolls, vases of every size and shape, quantities of eggshell china, a set of sleigh bells, a bushel of artificial flowers, many yards of lace and goodness knows what else.

There is still some argument whether the Barnsley plunder was a bargain, though a few pieces of the jade were worth the purchase price of the entire tonnage. The woman's argument in such matters is that if you don't want jade jewelry it isn't cheap at any price.

There was never any serious argument about my collection of stone jars, jugs and bean pots, some of which still adorn the high shelves of the library. I never spent much money for them. I can still grieve, in fact, because I once let a tall pitcher of brown stoneware get away from me when its price passed ten cents. Twenty years ago it was a poor country sale that did not include a few crocks and bean pots. Common, too, were the tall jars and pitchers decorated with blue leaves and flower patterns in crude slip ware, and ten cents was considered plenty to pay for them.

I suppose I have picked up fifty or more in my time. We have made some use of them, enough to deplete the collection seriously by breakage. We used to put fresh eggs away in them for winter storage in "water glass." During the prohibition era some held fearful and wonderful concoctions intended to become wine, which usually turned out to be vinegar. We have even baked beans in a gallon bean pot, probably made a century ago and bought at a Bucks County auction sale for a dime.

There is no sense in baking beans in a bean pot, even though you bake them in a brick oven at the back of an old farmhouse fireplace. Better beans come out of cans. Many other old-fashioned foodstuffs are better store-bought than homemade, though Henry Tetlow's book, *We Farm for a Hobby*, will flatly tell you different. There are hooks in my cellar for the hanging of home-smoked hams, but I have no hankering to keep pigs and spoil their meat by home curing. They do that sort of thing better in Chicago.

It seems to me, indeed, that one of the few encouraging signs of human progress in these backsliding times is the slow emancipation of the womenfolk from enslavement to the cookstove. Final verdict on this point may depend on what they do with the time they save. But for a century past, the century in which my house has been standing, they have been getting away from it all in a rather big way. This was a transition period, for much of the stuff sold at these country sales was left over from days of kitchen slavery. Scrapple pans, pepper grinders, sausage-making machines, churns, nutmeg graters, butter molds, wash boilers, rolling pins and invariably an assortment of Mason jars, usually without lids or tops.

As concerns Mason jars and jelly glasses there is a mystery, perhaps a scandal. Every truly rural sale turned them up by dozens and hundreds. They came out of low-ceilinged and murky cellars, I suppose, like the spidery crypt which underlies my own house. And within a few years after we moved in we ourselves began to wonder where all the jars and jelly glasses came from.

Twenty, or even fifty, might be accountable. But when I was seized one day by desire to house-clean the cellar, a task not unlike that of Hercules in the Aegean stables, I found shelves and floor crowded with hundreds of them. They lurked in corners and huddled in dusty cupboards. I could surmise only one explanation. Jelly glasses must multiply by their own volition or by the operation of natural law; perhaps through process of amoebic separation or by some obscure biologic process or a sort of spontaneous generation. This could not happen in a modern cellar, where children play ping-pong while Father reads a good book and an antiseptic oil burner looks on with a silent and odorless smile. But ours is a brooding cellar, a stale and musty cellar, and strange things may happen there.

Many of these Mason jars and jelly tumblers came from country sales, but I swear I never meant to buy them. Neither did I intend to waste my substance on rusty meat axes, snaffle bits, tools for making holes in harness or barn forks without handles. But the rules of the country sale were rigid.

XIII. Why Wives Leave Home

Everything must be sold and somebody must buy it. You might look innocent of all ambition to bid or buy, but the auctioneer would declare you the highest bidder for five cents' worth of scrap iron or kitchen rubbish, and you must take it and like it. Or else, when you bid for something you wanted, he would neither see nor hear you.

So the Lady of the House would break into tears, sometimes, to see what lay on the front porch when I unloaded the car or wagon after a session at a country sale. Sometimes she went to the sale in self-defense, but not very successfully. Two kinds of women attended sales in those days. There were those from the rural regions who had been brought up on auction sales and could make up their minds in a moment what they wanted and how much to pay for it. And there were the innocents who tortured themselves with uncertainties while bargains got away or lost all sense of values in a wild scramble of competition. Nothing better pleased the auctioneer, who was paid by percentage, than two women bidding up a secondhand bureau to the price of a new one.

Keeping a clear head at a country sale wasn't easy anyway. At Trevose, about 1920, I got an old four-poster bed for fifteen cents. I suppose it was an antique. It had knobs to hold a lattice of rope, in lieu of spring, and a scrolled headboard. I had hardly bought it before a strange woman wanted it. She wanted it fifty cents' worth. Ten minutes earlier I had thought fifteen cents plenty for the bed; now it seemed suddenly valuable. The lady raised her price to $1.00. I couldn't imagine selling for such a trifling sum. The bid went up to $3.50, and still I wouldn't sell.

I should have taken the money and let her have her four-poster. The bed wasn't any good, except for fifteen cents' worth of firewood.

Partly the passion for American antiques seems to have burned itself out; partly the racket has been ruined by putting fancy prices on furniture whose only real distinction is that it is old enough to know better. The purchasing public has grown suspicious too, as it should be. It is old stuff in Bucks County to put a piece of antique furniture casually on a farmhouse porch and wait for some city sucker to see it and want it. If he buys it, the farmer climbs to the attic and gets out more bait.

By painful trial and error, moreover, many people have found out that a piece of furniture, or anything else, is not necessarily valuable because it is aged and decrepit. A lot of the furniture of our forefathers was poorly

My Own Four Walls

made and miserably designed for comfort. Some of it could serve no reasonable purpose in modern use. I could never understand, for example, why the antique collectors grabbed greedily for a clumsy chair which had been made over for the comfort of somebody's great-grandmother in her helpless old age. I cannot detect the special beauty or value in an ancient kitchen table which my sons could build better in their manual-training classes. And many other Americans have learned by now, I imagine, that wormholes are really attractive only to a worm and that all that is chipped is not Chippendale.

But twenty years ago the women, in particular, went after antiques in our neighborhood with a grim and unreasoning energy. Two of them came one day to our door. They wanted to know if we had any antiques. The Lady of the House said she didn't think so; certainly we had none for sale. The visitors by this time had edged inside the door and cast appraising eyes over our poor possessions. Their faces gleamed with joyful greed to see a tall Seth Thomas clock on the mantel. One of its decorative pineapples was missing; the glass was cracked and the clock ten minutes slow. Plainly an antique, and we too poor and innocent to do it honor.

The visiting ladies, with transparent cunning, took a liking to the clock. They said they would buy the clock for $10, maybe $15, and we could get ourselves a nice new one. It was said that the clock was not for sale. The ladies went out, conferred in whispers and came back to offer $25.

So it was necessary to tell them that the clock was a pretty good reproduction of an old Seth Thomas, purchased new at Fred Cooper's store for $35, and that its damages came not of age but of the fact that young Sylvia tried one day to wind the clock and pulled it down on her head. It would have served them right to have sold them the clock.

Best bargain of my buying at country sales was apparently a totally useless purchase. This was a wagon bought at Newt Branin's obituary sale in the summer of 1934.

The wagon caused a certain amount of consternation in our community. I found it out when taking the morning train to town a few days later. An acquaintance came right out with it. "Where are you going to keep your horse?" he wanted to know.

Neighbors are fond of jumping at conclusions, usually unpleasant

XIII. Why Wives Leave Home

ones. By long experience I have also found out that there's nothing gained by denying gossip. The thing to do is to admit it, which usually puts an end to it. But on this occasion I stared right back at him and asked, "What horse?"

It appeared that rumor was raging through the village that I had bought a wagon at the Branin sale and was hard on the heels of a horse to fit it.

I had bought the wagon, all right, but had no thought of buying a horse. At early afternoon the auctioneer had worked his way through an assortment of farmyard machinery while I followed along for the fun of it. There were plows and harrows, a cider press, a racing sulky, sleighs and carts, two grindstones and the rigging and timbers of a well.

Midway along the line there stood an ancient vehicle. It was faded and forlorn, its shafts drooped dejectedly, its seat was tattered and torn. By Blue Book rating its market worth was about $15 less than nothing. Yet I knew at once that it must be mine. In swift survey I noted that it still had four wheels, one whipsocket and a lantern hook at the rear. What wagon needs more?

The auctioneer wasted no time or compliments on the ancient equipage. He faked a first bid of fifty cents. "Seventy-five," says I. "Sold," says he.

Our village has seen some pretty fine parades on the Fourth of July. None would bear comparison with the triumphant procession which escorted and accompanied the wagon to its new home, hitched by ropes to the rear of the family car. On the wagon seat, high and handsome above the envious crowd, rode two boys who could have been Tom Sawyer and Huck Finn in person. One of them, now grown to a man's estate and the illustrator of this book, had been whitewashing the house that morning and had finished the job by falling off the ladder ahead of the whitewash bucket. The bucket and whitewash caught up with him.

In fifteen minutes there was hardly a small boy within miles who hadn't heard about the wagon and was either riding in it or hauling it. By eventide reservations for the use of the wagon were booked three days ahead.

So the wagon needed no horse, nor ever had one after I owned it. The wagon represented an investment of seventy-five cents in juvenile

enjoyment and paid generous dividends for a year or two. It is significant that the younger generation of modern America was so well pleased with it. When the wagon arrived the demand for automobile rides shrank to nothing. Airplanes and autogiros could fly overhead and never be noticed. For these were merely machinery, while this was an honest-to-goodness wagon, with four wheels and a whipsocket and everything. Or nearly everything, except a horse.

It needed considerable research to identify the wagon. Some said it was just a spring wagon. Somebody spoke of it as a Democrat wagon, assuming that it had low board sides, which it didn't. Finally the milkman, Joe Conard, took one look at it and named it. He said it was a spindle buggy.

The spindle buggy was called many other things before it was done with. It was a covered wagon crossing the Western plains, an armored tank, a ten-ton truck. Turned on its side, its big rear wheel made a fair enough merry-go-round.

It is remembered among the most appreciated playthings the youngsters ever enjoyed. And having once owned a spindle buggy and a large family, but no horse, I know exactly what a wagonload of fun looks like.

XIV

Handy Man Around the House

Probably I share the title of "handy man around the house" with a majority of those entangled in matrimony. Most of us got this way without fair warning, for neither the Christian nor civil ceremony of marriage says a word about it.

So the average bridegroom on his wedding day, being in a condition which cries aloud for deception and illusion, surveys unmoved the three electric irons, the coffeepot and toaster that loom so large and shiny among the wedding presents. He does not see the specter of the screw driver that hides behind them or the phantom of the pliers and monkey wrench gnashing their teeth in gleeful anticipation. With equal innocence he leads his bride into a new house, and together they rejoice in its Renaissance electric-light fixtures, Dutch-tiled bathroom, English breakfast nook, colonial mantel, Italian library and Spanish porch. They are all new and beautiful, and it is incredible that they can ever come apart and need patching and mending.

But they will. The fundamental fact about houses and all that is within them is that they fall to pieces. So does everything else, with the small exception of the Pyramids perhaps, but the lares and penates of light housekeeping seem peculiarly susceptible to change and decay. The newest home in your neighborhood is already in the shadow of the wrecker's hammer, though its optimistic occupant may not know it. And his new radio and refrigerator are wearing out already, even though they are not yet paid for.

This may be the penalty of progress and the price of civilization. The

My Own Four Walls

savage in his bamboo hut knows nothing about fixing a leaking spigot. The heathen in his blindness knows nothing of glazing broken windows. The Eskimo in his cold-storage establishment need never empty the pan beneath the icebox. The fish in the sea and the birds in their nests and the amoebas in their little protoplasms are rarely interrupted in their evolutionary progress by a broken belt or busted wringer on a washing machine.

All of which indicates that evolution has been very carelessly handled to date and will eventually have to be done over again. For the handy man around the house, though almost essential to middle-class living, is a phenomenon that was certainly never contemplated in the cradle of the race, over in the suburbs of Abyssinia.

In the big cities there are exceptions to the rule requiring a handy man around the house in every happy home. The apartment dweller dodges his share of the white man's burden. For there is rarely room in an apartment for a handy man around the house, which is one reason why people who live in apartments are usually somewhere else.

The genuine handy man is a suburbanite and homeowner; he pays tribute to railroads and building associations; he counts his weeks by the coming of the garbage collector on Wednesdays and light exercise with the lawn mower on Saturday afternoons, and his months by the visits of the man who reads the meters. He is, or should be, a compendium of useful information and a cross section of the mechanical trades. He is also a slave to the environment which he himself has created.

There have been times when I have envied the philosophy of my friend and neighbor, Randolph Childs, a lawyer by profession and wise in other matters than the law. Mr Childs made up his mind some years ago that he is physically and mentally incapable of fixing things. When a sink spigot leaks the only remedy he knows is to put a bucket beneath it. When the toaster breaks down he prefers plain bread and butter for breakfast. If the vacuum cleaner won't work he buys his wife a new one.

But when we settled in our farmhouse I chose the harder way. Under the influence of handy men who had lived there before, I endeavored to make myself master of the so-called labor-saving machinery which clutters up a modern household. I also resolved that I could manage to mend anything that could fall apart.

So in the years of my schoolteaching much of my vacation time was

XIV. Handy Man Around the House

taken up with repairs and reclamation work. Some days I plumbed, wrenching at pipes and working wonders with washers. Sometimes I electrocuted, tinkering with wires and fuses and shocking myself and the family. On Wednesdays I carpentered, mended furniture and hung wash lines in new places. On Thursdays I masoned, patched plaster and laid bricks. On Fridays I glazed and was rarely more than three windows in back of the children's playful habit of breaking them. On Saturdays I did general janiting and renewed my stocks of tools and hardware. On Sundays I went to church and needed it.

I met my Waterloo, and also two Balaklavas and a Flodden Field, when I resolved to rebuild and upholster the living-room couch.

The life of an ordinary piece of furniture coincides roughly with that of the time payments which purchase it, but may be modified by the number and activity of the children who use it. Three or four children are fatal in short order to overstuffed furniture of all sorts. Five mean the early end of wicker chairs. Six will send solid oak and walnut into a rapid decline; nine or more will be too much and too many for mission chairs and tables, not to mention cast-iron lawn furniture.

Our overstuffed couch was an excellent example of the workings of this natural law. It was a good couch when young, but by the time the fourth baby began to climb it was in a seriously run-down condition. It was lame in one leg and propped precariously with an anthology of English poetry. Its geography had undergone a sort of seismic convulsion. There were mountain peaks and ridges in it, valleys and sinkholes. It also had leaked. During its years of hard service it had leaked several bales of hay and excelsior—sufficient to insulate a small ice-house. As I looked it over it seemed reasonably certain that it was nothing but the hollow shell of its former self.

So I resolved to remove it to the workshop and remodel it there to a fashionable figure. But I discovered that it could not be got out of the room. It came in, but it wouldn't go out. It had evidently settled and spread and stiffened with age and would no longer turn a corner or go sideways through a door.

So we moved it to the center of the room, effectively blocking traffic in all directions, and proceeded with the problem of dismantling it.

The first thing was to remove the cushions, which discovered an

My Own Four Walls

astonishing collection of domestic debris. There were three pairs of scissors, nine pencils, one buttonhook, eleven spoons and three cents. This was an unexpected dividend on our good intentions, so we went cheerfully ahead and took the cover off. At the first breach all the insides fell out.

Nobody could imagine why the manufacturer should have put a ton of chopped hay into a stuffed couch, but there it was. All that had fallen out before made no difference to the final catastrophe. The room was full of it. But we shoveled it away and stripped the couch grimly down to its naked skeleton, consisting chiefly of helical springs tied with three miles of string, all tangled in hundreds of Gordian knots. Removing these, we found we had nothing left except about fifteen cents' worth of box lumber and three castors.

Now there was nothing to do but put the couch together again, contriving somehow to get all the springs back in place and hold them in place while they were tied here and there, fore and aft, coming and going. It was at this moment that we agreed that we should have bought a new couch. Later on we were sure of it, when we discovered that the springs left their mark on any unfortunate who sat down on the couch. It made no difference that they were padded with old blankets, soft shirts and absorbent cotton; they were still there.

But we went bravely on, having come so far, and attempted to nail the new cover on. You may have noticed that on a properly upholstered piece of overstuffed furniture none of the nails show. They are all inside. We were frankly puzzled to know how they get there. But at last I figured it out.

When the frame of a couch or chair is completed in the furniture factory a small boy is placed inside with a handful of nails and hammer and proceeds to nail the cover on from the inside. The couch or chair is then removed to a room known as the Drying Department and left there until the boy dries up and can be shaken out through the slats at the bottom. The hammer and extra nails are recovered in the same fashion.

Since we valued our children and could borrow none from the neighbors with sufficient sense and breeding to hit a nail with a hammer, I was obliged to nail the cover on from the outside. It looked terrible and eventually most of the nails pulled out. They were hammered in again, but meanwhile the cover had stretched so seriously that there were hanging

XIV. Handy Man Around the House

jowls all over it. For a while we took tucks and pleats to it, but at last I took an ax to it.

It was my hardly won reputation as a handy man around the house which entrapped me in the building of extra closet space. Early American architects had a fixed idea that two closets were plenty for anybody's household. So we have spent twenty-two years looking for places to put more closets. It is a tough problem to bring up a large family on two closets and a few hooks, and may never be solved completely until the kids grow up, get married and move out.

It's all very well to tell children to put their things away when they've finished with them, but where shall they put them in a house with only two closets? In the hall closet, of course, on top of my rubbers.

The hall closet is an oversight of the original builders of the house, or else they found some space beneath the stairs and couldn't think what else to do with it. It is a large closet, as closets go in our house, and is mainly filled with the incredible quantities of overcoats, sweaters, leggings, hats, gloves and overshoes which are considered minimum requirement for a modern family. And my rubbers are in there, when I want them, if I could only imagine some way of getting at them.

I could get down on hands and knees and crawl into the closet and hunt for them. Sure I could, and when I was well inside all the coats and wraps would fall on me and smother me. Or somebody would shut the door. It is an early American door, with a latch on the outside and no way out on the inside. That makes the hall closet a convenient place to put a child when he's naughty and then go away and forget all about him.

When my wife dies she hopes to go to heaven and live in a house that is half closets at least. And we have both wondered, while looking for another place to put a hook, what the aboriginal Americans did for closet and cupboard space. They used oversized wardrobes, I know, and the rest of the explanation must be that two suits of clothes were considered enough for any man and three dresses for his wife.

So I have built several closets, here and there, and have my eye on space for another when the second daughter gets married and has a house of her own to hang her clothes in. By which time, perhaps, we won't need another closet.

My Own Four Walls

One of my earliest adventures in handiness around the house was a little job of plastering a hole in the ceiling. Plastering looks easy, especially when somebody else is doing it. I had watched plasterers laying it on a square foot at one sweep, and there seemed no good reason why I should not do likewise.

For practice I did a few patches on the wall, and it was no trouble at all. The effect was a little lumpy, but I pointed out that the wallpaper would cover most of it. Then I climbed on a scaffold consisting of the kitchen table and two chairs and applied some plaster to the bare laths of the ceiling. It went on easily and fell off immediately.

Everybody laughed heartily. So I scooped up the plaster and tried again. With a little more pressure and a great deal more plaster, most of which disappeared between the laths, I managed to cover the bald spot. Then we removed the scaffolding and everybody admired my work. Suddenly somebody shouted, "Look out!" Before anything could be done about it the plaster bulged like a balloon or blister, wabbled awhile and fell on the floor with a sickening thud.

I fought for hours with that patch of plaster. I would get it up and it would pretend it was going to stay there. But as soon as I turned my back it unstuck itself and fell to the floor. I finished the job, finally, by holding it to the ceiling until it hardened and couldn't fall off if it tried.

Since then I have learned that the correct consistency of plaster for patching a ceiling is as critical as the mixing of batter for good buckwheat cakes. But science has stepped in, both on behalf of pancakes and plaster, and ready-mixed materials can now be purchased in packages.

There are infinite opportunities for a handy man around the house to exercise his talents, and many books have been written on the subject. Some cover every emergency from grass stains on white flannel trousers to the installation of downspouts and gutters. But the basis of all household handiness is a decent collection of tools, a place to keep them and a disciplinary system which will prevent small children from swiping and losing them.

Hammer and saw are essential. Thrift calls for knowing how to set and sharpen a saw, and I hope to learn how someday, probably when old age makes it impossible for the screech of metal to set my teeth on edge. There must be screw divers, chisels, a wrench or two, planes, pliers and

XIV. Handy Man Around the House

a nail punch. Added to these should be a good vise. Not a cheap and ordinary vice, like smoking or swearing, but something with teeth in it.

All these and more I have collected in my cellar workshop, a happy winter refuge from the slings and arrows of family life upstairs. The Lady of the House approves my workshop, though not all the craftsmanship which comes out of it. A wise woman doesn't care much where her husband is, but she wants to know where he is. If he's safely down cellar she has nothing to worry about.

Down in the workshop, on a bench built of two obsolete and abandoned washing-machine frames, I have made and mended many things. A notable undertaking of recent memory was a small roof, or shelter, to shed rain water away from the back door. It was a neat job, if I say so myself, ingeniously designed to be completed in one piece and afterwards fastened over the kitchen door. I finished it in three happy evenings and then found it was three inches too wide to get out of the cellar.

So as a handy man around the house, both in respect to alterations and repairs, I have been through the mill and also the meat grinder and am roughly holding my own as the old house crumbles and its internal machinery falls apart. But lately I have begun to take advantage of the fact that near at hand is a telephone, which I have never been required to repair, and within its range are dozens of mechanics who will cheerfully leave their firesides to repair my household comforts and conveniences at a cost not much in excess of that of rebuilding and refurnishing the whole establishment. After twenty-five years of it, perhaps, a man may be permitted to pick and choose among his domestic employments. My choice, in more recent years, has been for the garden crafts of brickwork, masonry and floriculture rather than those of the workbench.

The confirming comment on my experience as a handy man around the house came from the lips of a child too young to lie about it. It was young Donette, then four years old, who paid innocent tribute to my handiness with tools in domestic service.

She is, and was, an observant youngster. Among other things she must have noticed that whenever I was home I was quite likely to be busy repairing something—down in an attitude of prayer before the old family washing machine, trying to find out why the sweeper wouldn't sweep and the toaster wouldn't toast or otherwise fixing some household equipment that needed fixing.

We were looking over a picture book together. "What's that, Donette?" I asked her.

"After all these years," said Donette to herself, "he doesn't know a horse when he sees one," and told me it was a horsie. Similarly she identified a piggie, pussy and doggie. We came to a farmyard scene, with chickens and cows and the hired man milking a cow.

"What's that, Donette?" I asked her.

"That's chickies," said Donette, "and a cow, and a man fixing the cow."

XV

Bricks Are So Plentiful

Do you happen to have a brick or two around the house or garden which you aren't using? Of course you do. Everybody has a brick. The smallest suburban home, the tiniest of city gardens, the emptiest of vacant lots and the ugliest community dump have a brick or two lying around somewhere.

I believe I could drive a wagon through any typical American village, town or city suburb, crying "Bring out your bricks," and come home with sufficient assorted bricks to build a small barn.

I have never thought of building a brick barn but frequently of laying brick pavements. There is no better way of bordering a garden than with bricks. Their warm red color, speckled with green of moss and lichens, is the perfect foundation for a pattern of flowers in bloom. They walk well in wet or dry weather and they don't track mud in the house.

When I planned my first pavement I did so under the delusion that the house, garden and adjacent landscape were glutted with bricks. There seemed to be bricks all over the place. There was a brick in the coat closet beneath the stairs and another on the front porch, vaguely intended for small boys to scrape their shoes on before entering the house. There were a lot of bricks scattered around the cellar. Now and then I fell over a brick in the flower garden or blackberry patch. I remembered a brick in the laundry and a brick blocking a rathole in the outside kitchen. I would have said, in fact, that there were fifty bricks lying around the place, if not five hundred.

When fully prepared to lay a pavement I collected the bricks. There were eleven of them.

It is difficult to believe that eleven bricks can seem so many when

My Own Four Walls

scattered about a house and garden and so pitifully few when laid in a brick pavement where they belong. Eleven bricks make less than three square feet of pavement, and three feet are hardly a beginning. And so the pavement, for lack of bricks, was stopped before it was well started.

After that, though, I began to see bricks wherever I went in my travels. I found out that the great city of Philadelphia, in its domestic sections, is largely made of brick. So are parts of the central city that have slid down the social scale from colonial days to slumhood. At that time their owners were tearing brick houses down by dozens to dodge taxes, turning the vacant lots into parking places. Many streets of Philadelphia had gaps like missing teeth in a grinning mouth.

And everywhere were bricks, neatly piled or sprawling on the sites of vanished buildings. Millions of bricks. In vast numbers nobody seemed to own them, nobody seemed to want them. Where they lay they were worthless, or nearly, and could be had for the taking. All I needed to do was to figure out some economical and inconspicuous way of getting them from where they were to where they ought to be.

That is how I happened to run head on into that old public enemy, the problem of distribution of natural resources. It applies not only to bricks. On farms in the Red Hills of Pennsylvania I have seen such quantities of stone, suitable for all sorts of purposes in a walled and terraced garden, as would keep me out of mischief for the rest of my horticultural life. But stones and garden are sixty miles apart, and a load of stone, in our village, costs $3.00. And a load of fireplace wood costs more than that, though the woods a few miles away are full of fallen trees.

Something ought to be done about it. Yet all the wisdom of mankind, to date, has not discovered how to move a brick from where it isn't wanted to my back yard without kiting the cost of the brick to three times its true value. It might be done, perhaps, as a project for relief of unemployment. Thousands of men could be put to work carrying bricks, one at a time, to relieve the surplus in the crumbling cities and supply the needs of the garden-loving and bricklaying suburbs.

Or else I could carry home a brick or two every day on my way from work in the city. It would hurt nobody very much if I helped myself to a brick now and then from the plethora of the vacant lots.

The idea did not work out well. American policemen are lenient with

XV. Bricks Are So Plentiful

traffic offenders. They can bear it if a citizen beats his wife or sells lottery tickets. They can comfortably ignore a variety of illegal and lethal rackets. But they soon wake up and take notice if a man tries to borrow a brick.

The law was always looking if I planned to pick an abandoned brick from a pile and walk quietly away. And even though I got away with it, it arouses a lot of public curiosity if you carry a brick through the crowds at the rush hour. Carry it casually as you please, pretending you are a brick salesman with a sample or a bricklayer on the way to work, but you still attract attention.

Even in the comparative privacy of suburban and rural highways there are bricks, waifs and strays at the wayside, waiting to be carried away and laid in a pavement. I found two fine bricks only half a mile from home. Under ordinary circumstances that section of the highway is deserted. But because I was carrying bricks I met nearly everybody I knew before I was home, including ladies to whom I tried to raise my hat, a convulsive undertaking when you are carrying two large and heavy bricks.

At last I had twoscore bricks, not nearly enough to make a pavement. And I had found out that buying bricks was out of the financial question. I needed not less that a thousand bricks, and if I paid the market price I would not have had the heart to walk on them, nor shoes either.

My gainful employment, for some years, has been that of daily columnist for the *Evening Public Ledger* of Philadelphia. The column, called "Stuff and Nonsense," is not one of these pontifical affairs devoted to politics, economics or social problems. It plows the foothills of Parnassus for much smaller potatoes. Its customary themes, according to the *Ledger*'s own advertising about it, are "the familiar absurdities of average existence, the lights and shadows of the domestic comedy, the fads and follies of American life and custom." The definition, as you see, can easily be stretched to cover a brick shortage in a back garden.

One dull day I wrote a few paragraphs dealing with the lamentable lack of bricks in some places and the surplus in others. Shortly after the first edition hit the sidewalk somebody walked across the street with a brick picked up from a house-wrecking job. By eventide several wastepaper baskets of bricks had been delivered to my desk.

Next morning many bricks came by mail; others by messenger. There

My Own Four Walls

were red, black and white bricks; whole bricks and half bricks. In a week there were two hundred bricks on the desk, floor and bookcases.

I suspected a conspiracy and would not be surprised if Charley Polk, the paper's star political reporter, had an instigating hand in it. From his home town in New Jersey came four wrapped packages which were held at the post office for $4.25 postage due. They had been mailed at parcel-post rates, though containing both bricks and letters. And I warn you never to attempt evasion of the law by putting letters in parcel-post packages. Postal employees have X-ray eyes or else can smell a letter wrapped with a brick.

The post-office people asked whether I would pay the postage and claim my packages. I said they could keep them and build a new post office. A few years later they did build a new post office.

The bricks went home, finally, in the family car. Many others were delivered at the house, and one contributor, through overloading his flivver with all the bricks in his back yard, paid for his kindness with a busted spring. A stranger stopped at the door one day to turn in a brick picked up on a Georgia highway. Another drove forty miles from upstate to bring a brick. A brick beautifully silver-plated with aluminum paint was presented by one of the local Rotary clubs.

All in all, about six hundred bricks were donated toward what is now called the Pilgrims' Pavement in disrespectful imitation of the floor of a famous cathedral in New York City. Mine is not a very beautiful pavement. It wanders vaguely at the back of the house, about twenty feet of it, and there must be seventeen kinds of bricks in it. But every brick has its personal history, if I could remember it.

Contributors to the Pilgrims' Pavement come calling sometimes on Sunday afternoons and want to see where their brick is laid. Fortunately, few of them remember what kind of brick it was. So I point confidently to almost any old brick and say, "There's your brick." Usually they are very pleased and go away promising to bring more bricks.

For the rest of the brickwork, of which there is a great deal around the garden, I bought secondhand bricks. Some are plain bricks and some are fancy firebricks, discarded when a big heating plant was torn down. Even at a third of their original price bricks are shockingly expensive. So that when I find myself in the financial doldrums I can wander in the

XV. Bricks Are So Plentiful

garden, contemplate ten thousand bricks and know where all the money goes.

At one time I contemplated cutting expenses by offering a dime a dozen for all bricks delivered at the door by small boys of the neighborhood, with no questions asked. The scheme was working splendidly until it was bruited abroad through Bryn Athyn that the boys were tearing down walls, chimneys and porches to turn an honest dime or two. But it would work well enough, I think, in a city neighborhood where stray bricks are plentiful and a public nuisance.

Bricklaying is considered one of the skilled trades, and I sometimes wonder why. It must be because some people find it difficult to lay one brick on top of another in accordance with the laws of geometry and the

My Own Four Walls

rules of the union. And I admit that it may call for a straight eye on the job, not to mention a straight face on payday, to build a brick wall that is true and plumb and neatly pointed, which is not the kind of wall I build.

But if you are not too particular it is little trouble to build a brick wall. You begin by laying down a brick and then another beyond it, so that one end of one brick is contiguous with one end of the other brick, leaving the other ends of both bricks as far apart as possible under the circumstances. Repeat the process with a third brick. Lay two bricks on top of the three bricks, so that each of the two upper bricks spans the joint between two of the lower bricks. Lay a third brick on top of the two bricks which are on top of the three bricks. That makes six bricks in all, and it is now lunch time.

Mortar must also be taken into consideration. Mortar is made of sand and cement and water and should be mixed by somebody else if possible. The mortar serves a double purpose in a wall. On one hand it holds the bricks together; on the other it keeps them apart. It takes long practice to persuade mortar to stay on the trowel while you put it where it belongs, but few accomplishments are so richly rewarded in personal satisfaction. A famous prime minister of England, a man of parts and genius, was proudest of all of his ability to lay a brick without spilling mortar in the cuffs of his trousers.

It is even easier than building a wall to lay a brick pavement or terrace. It is a wise and thrifty thing to do, moreover, if your garden has been mainly a blackberry patch for fifty years or so, as was ours when we bought it. Blackberries are among the most stubborn of vegetables and will sprout again from the roots though you chop them down continually. But a blackberry cane gets discouraged and quits when it bumps into a brick.

So there is a wide brick terrace where the blackberries used to be, a pleasant spot for summer breakfasts and for watching the sunset through the weeping willow. It is shaded by two parasol trees. You will not find the parasol tree mentioned in books of aboriculture, because a parasol tree is a black walnut, planted by a squirrel laying up store for the winter, which has been kept topped and trimmed to an umbrella shape.

Flowering perennials surround the terrace and some smaller stuff, forget-me-nots, poppies and Johnny-jump-ups, which are agreeable garden guests because they attend to their own seeding. Their weakness in

XV. Bricks Are So Plentiful

this respect is that they would sooner seed themselves between bricks than anywhere else. It may be assumed that the bricks shelter them through the long hard winter, and with the coming of spring they sprout in every crevice.

So do weeds of every kind. A weed will grow anywhere but loves best to wind its tendrils around a terrace brick. And as I weed the terrace on bended knee I can philosophize, if I feel like it, on the resemblance of weeds to the stubborn wickedness of mankind, including all sorts of sins and bad habits. By taking thought you may rid yourself of one of them, but two sprout in its place.

It is much the same with weeds. No weed dies without a successor; it passes on the torch. The dandelions come and go but do not leave a vacancy. After them come the plantains, the mustard, the chickweed. These droop and die, and on their heels are the ragweed, matweed and milkweed. Last, but not least, is the mighty burdock, monarch of all weeds that grow. What a weed! What stout and meaty stalks, what leathery leaves, what lengthy roots and clinging seeds!

Well, it is a pleasure to report that something has been done, at last, about weeds. The stuff has a trade name, but I suspect it is mainly saltpeter. You spray its solution on the weeds, especially poison ivy, and the saltpeter filters through leaf and stalk to the uttermost tip of the root. And no weed will grow there again for a long time. It is the only treatment, in this busy and harassed world, which will keep a brick terrace in reasonable neatness and repair without more trouble than the task is worth.

The brick terrace surrounds a strange little garden, guarded by ivied walls, whose existence is one of the surviving mysteries of my estate. Its walls were there when we came, buried by blackberry canes, and within them was a dump and rubbish heap that must have taken decades to accumulate. We added to it through the years, until the slow encroachments of civilization crowded out the blackberry patch and came upon the half-buried stonework. I dug eight or ten feet into the rubbish and could not reach the bottom of the walls. They were set in iron-hard mortar, moreover, and could not be torn down for the stone in them.

So I built them up instead and made a garden of them, suitable for serving tea and cocktails. Much speculation has been wasted on them since then. For the walls are built in a rough diamond shape, no two of the same length, so that no two angles are the same. Once there was a roof over them, and it must have been a tricky job of carpentering to put it there. There was formerly a door and window to the place, but what was it?

It could have been a smokehouse or icehouse, without which no early American farmyard was well equipped. Why it was so oddly built I do not know, nor does anybody else.

My ambitions, from the beginning, have included a sunken garden. I have my sunken garden by accident and by operation of the laws of change and decay. Under the bricks and borders of the little garden lies an incredible assortment of the detritus of light housekeeping. But the dead cats are slowly dissolving into original chaos; the tin cans are crumbling and the discarded mattresses disintegrating. So the garden is going down, and I do not know where or when it will stop. This is a unique feature of my horticultural surroundings, for there are very few sunken gardens in existence that are still doing it.

XVI

Are You a Mason?

Among the ancient skills and handicrafts my choice would not be carpentry or plumbing. My preferred hobby is for tinkering with a trowel. Not the common or garden trowel, but the kind used by masons and plasterers. When I am extremely rich and lazy I should like to own a large collection of trowels, just as some men get great satisfaction out of an assortment of firearms or fishing rods. There will be large trowels and little trowels, square trowels and triangular trowels, pointing trowels and smoothing trowels. Hawkins, the manservant, will come to the bedside at a decent hour of midmorning, wake me gently and murmur, "Which trowel today, sir?"

For I find it the most soothing of all domestic employments to lay a bit of wall or patch of pavement. When the world totters toward chaos, when life is cruel and friends forgetful, when the cup of grief is full and the bank account empty, there is sweet relief in messing about with a favorite trowel and a bucket of obedient mortar.

Perhaps it is only the mud-pie impulse of infancy, revived by the dawning of a second childhood, which makes me want to lay a brick or fit stones together in the pattern of a wall. Or it may be a more profound creative urge, demanding to leave its mark on something that will endure. For it is a little shocking to realize how much of our labors leaves no visible mark or memorial. Even the job whereby we earn our living is ephemeral as doing the dinner dishes or washing a small boy's face. Whatever we do today must be done again tomorrow. But a wall will stay together, if well built, much longer than the man who builds it.

Sometimes I have suspected that early Latin studies account for my masonic instincts and ambitions. I started learning Latin in an English board school at the age of twelve. I don't remember much about it, except

that *Balbus murum aedificavit.* Forty years ago the study of elementary Latin was largely devoted to Balbus' efforts to build a wall and his brother's jeering at the job he made of it. Balbus built a wall. The brother of Balbus jumped over the wall. Balbus killed his brother for belittling his wall. There were innumerable variations on the theme, involving sundry Latin moods and tenses and a steadily enlarging vocabulary.

Possibly it is my adolescent acquaintance with Balbus which makes me prefer wall building to any other outdoor hobby. My friends prefer golf, fishing, tennis or pitching horseshoes. But they are American born and educated and don't know about Balbus.

XVI. Are You a Mason?

It is probably useless to attempt to share my masonic enthusiasms with those who have never known the joy of a neat job of pointing. They could never understand my admiration for a really good concrete mixer. Neither do I much envy or admire the man who spends his spare time smacking a little white ball into a hole in the ground, over a course of traps and bunkers deliberately designed to be more trouble than they are worth. Life has difficulties enough without inventing a lot of additional hazards and perplexities and calling them golf.

You may remember the chap in Wordsworth's poem who didn't appreciate primroses. "A primrose by the river's brim a yellow primrose was to him, and it was nothing more." It has been argued that's all it was anyway, but the point of the poem is that Peter Bell wasn't genuinely interested in primroses. It's the same way about rocks with people who have never built a wall. They regard them as nothing more than rocks and not very interesting.

But when you have built a wall you begin to consider every stone you meet with a calculating eye. You recognize it as a good rock for a cornerstone or keystone. You notice that nature has designed it for a flagstone path or squared it nicely for the capstone of a corner. And you wonder, maybe, whether you could lift it quietly into the back of the car and get away without being seen.

Round and about my garden there are a hundred yards of wall and not less than a hundred and fifty stone steps. There is the vault or springhouse, the terraced rock garden and the outdoor fireplace. There is a lily pool and sundry varieties of pavement.

Visitors wonder where all the stone came from. And so, sometimes, do I. A lot of it came out of the burned and ruined barn. A few wagonloads were discarded stone from the building of the Bryn Athyn Cathedral. Some was the kindly gift of Victor Rosenquist, who bought one of the local quarry holes and is rapidly filling it with the rubbish of a neighboring township. Before the heap grew mountain-high I got away with a few tons of stone.

Some comes of my own digging and delving. The ancients who built my house did it mainly with stones gathered from their fields. They did not get them all, and wherever I dig deep I may find a small boulder. It is one of the house and garden rules that stones of any size may not be carelessly tossed aside. They must be piled together until the spirit moves me again to build a wall.

Other stones came from far and wide around the countryside. Many of them were collected at a time when we owned a prehistoric car named Polly Packard. Toward the twilight of her life Polly became famous by losing a door in fruitless argument with a telegraph pole and afterwards continued her erratic and uncertain career as the only three-door car in active service.

Advantages of a three-door car are many, and I wonder why the manufacturers do not build them that way. A three-door car is a safe car, demanding slow and careful driving, for it is difficult to drive it at more than thirty miles an hour without losing somebody out of the back seat. At fifty miles an hour they come out by twos and threes. Young children love a three-door car if permitted to sit in the space of the missing door, with their feet on the running board, and watch the passing show. There are other advantages of ventilation and of easy entrance and exit. But we found Polly particularly useful in collecting unwanted stones from rural roads and the creek valley. On a quiet and uncrowded evening we might take the car for a ride, find a few stones and accidentally lay them within the car. After which we drove home rapidly, turned the corner sharply into the drive, and the stones rolled out unaided.

This sort of thing may be regarded as conservation of natural resources. I am aware that some fussy landowners don't like strangers to swipe their rocks, but would be willing to argue that they should do something with their rocks or turn them over to somebody who will. What does it profit a rock to lie by the creekside for centuries when it might be doing service in a garden wall? What does it profit anybody?

My thriftiness in respect to rocks may come of my Anglican origins. In the latter years of my life in England we inhabited a dozen different homes in South London and its sprawling neighborhood. Few of them boasted more that a few square yards of garden space. Most of them, when we took possession, included an unpleasant corner where broken bottles, scrap iron and empty cans had crawled to die. Municipal facilities for disposing of such stuff, in those days, were vague and uncertain. So the garden-minded householder had small choice except to build a rockery above them.

XVI. Are You a Mason?

A rockery needs rocks. As a small boy, therefore, I could count on a special welcome home from school if I brought a stone with me. And with such stones my mother made marvelous rockeries, whose hidden core was rubbish.

Rockery builders swept the near countryside clean of loose stones, just as the woods of Europe are likely to be cleaned of the last twig that may make a fire beneath a kettle. And I am not quite accustomed, even now, to the prodigal plenty of the American countryside. Walking or driving anywhere beyond city limits, I see overwhelming quantities of stone and firewood, and no likely rock for a garden wall can consider itself safe if it lies within my reach.

Building stone has been providentially supplied, so far, as fast as I could make use of it. For the architectural achievements around the house are more than twenty years' work, and I see no prospect of finishing them altogether in less than another twenty. There are dates engraved in concrete and cement to prove it. The finishing touch on any job of paving or wall is to date the wet cement. So I know that the lower pavement was laid in 1922 under the skeptical eye of the contractor working on the rebuilding of the wheelwright's shop into a habitable cottage.

I was laying it on the bare earth, the cement work no thicker than the bricks which make patterns on the pavement. The contractor sneered that it wouldn't stay there through a single winter. It has been there nearly twenty years, because the date says so. So do some small footprints in its corner, which were put there by three children of tender years, now much larger than they used to be. One footprint, about four inches long, was put there by the illustrator of this volume, who now wears size 9½ shoes.

Elsewhere in the garden is recorded forever the evidence that he once studied French and it didn't take very well. He lent a helping hand to finish a flight of steps and a piece of paving at their top. I gave him license to adorn the top surface with small works of art. It must have been some years ago, because he included a swastika. At that time, apparently, the swastika had no sinister significance. It must have been early in the Roosevelt administration, because the centerpiece is the eagle of the N.R.A., with the motto "We Do Our Part." A border, or dado, seems to hint how we do our part.

It lists the names of the dozen youngsters who have called this house

My Own Four Walls

their home. "Tryn-Leon-Roy-Muriel-Stanley-Sylvia-Jack-Marjorie-Frank-Kenneth-Donette-Donald-Etc." The Etcetera was a precautionary postscript, but there isn't any Etcetera.

At the foot of a small flight of steps leading to the lawn the young man expressed himself in French. Deep in the cement he carved *Bon Chance*. It is a sad commentary on the elusiveness of popular education and the general condition of American culture that nobody found anything wrong with it for years after. It was Chief Caupolican, the Indian operatic baritone, who came out to sing at a local concert and gazed sadly at the imperishable inscription. "Luck is a lady," said he, "but you've made a man of her."

I have mentioned the skepticism of the contractor, which has been shared by many other professional masons and builders. They say my pavements should crack, my walls fall down. Some are annoyed that they don't.

The theory of professional masonry is that a wall must be footed two feet deep, below the frost line, and a pavement must be laid on a bed of loose cinders or something. This is an expensive hypothesis. Two feet of wall underground costs a lot of money and does nobody any good. Stone is too scarce and precious to bury.

By practice and experience I have given theory the lie. My methods would not work, perhaps, on anybody else's landscape. But the old farmhouse was built on a hillside, now terraced with walls and pavements. Water drains right through them, partly because they are loosely and even badly built. The effect is that when winter comes there is no water behind the walls or beneath the pavements to freeze and crack them apart. It is worth remembering, when you build a wall, that where there is no water there can be no ice.

Another matter which brings tears to the eyes of honest masons is my scandalous thriftiness with mortar. A professional mason, if he has his way, will build the smallest wall as though it were designed to support the Empire State Building. But a common or garden wall has nothing to carry but itself. So it needs no more mortar than enough to hold it together, which may be very little.

I claim invention of what I call the semidry wall. Building a real dry wall is a job for a skilled workman, and good dry wall builders are a

XVI. Are You a Mason?

vanishing tribe. The stones of a dry wall must be laid deep and fitted carefully. The semidry wall is a cheap and satisfactory substitute. Here and there you tie it together with coarse mortar and small stones. It may not stand for a century, but I know it will last for twenty years.

Another way to treat a retaining wall is to lay it dry and leave it for a year or two. By that time its stones will have shifted and settled and made themselves comfortable. They may bulge a bit, but a wall with bulges can be a good-looking wall. When it is decided that the stones are where they want to be you may fill its cracks and crevices with small stones and cement and have yourself a wall which looks solid all through. Perhaps it may crack some. If it cracks, smear it with a little more cement.

A course mortar, perhaps four parts of sand to one of cement, serves well enough for garden purposes. That kind of grout grows moss quickly if the wall faces northward, as do most of mine. In a season or two they are pleasantly patched with green and gray. Lime in mortar makes it easier to handle, but the moss doesn't seem to like lime.

I would recommend wall building without benefit of plumb or level. Around a house like mine, certainly, straight lines and true surfaces would be unseemly. The charm of old houses and gardens has much to do with their disregard for the plane and perpendicular. Imitating such artistic irregularity is something of a crime; it should come naturally of the mason's methods.

I have built most of my walls by squint and rule of thumb. The steps have been built where traffic demanded them. When the youngsters and neighbors establish a short cut across the lot you can shout at them, swear at them, put up notices and barriers. The wiser course is to take it that where traffic wants to go there should be a path for it to travel.

It is slow work, this masonry, but part of any sensible plan of living and playing is that a man must not work himself out of a job too soon. I have little envy of those with so much money that they buy their houses and gardens finished. After which they may walk in them but not work in them.

So for years to come, I hope, passers-by will be puzzled to see me still building walls and laying bricks. They may not understand that these are comforting employments, dulling the oversharp edge of thought and the complaining ache of conscience. They may not remember that Walt

My Own Four Walls

Whitman, poet of America, spoke very well of bricks, "each laid so workmanlike in its place and set with a knock of the trowel handle." They may not appreciate the pleasure of working with something that will stay where it is put long after the mason has laid aside his trowel.

"He made a chimney in my father's house," said Shakespeare, "and the bricks are alive at this day to testify it." The same goes for stones in a garden wall.

XVII

Laid on with a Trowel

"There is no ancient gentlemen but gardeners," said one of the gravediggers in *Hamlet*. It was Shakespeare, too, through the mouth of Celia in *As You Like It*, who acknowledged a neatly turned phrase with the comment, "That was laid on with a trowel." In modern idiom to lay it on with a trowel is to slice the bologna too thick or pour the oil of flattery too freely. Not so in the sixteenth century. Celia meant to say that her companion in conversation had expressed himself aptly, accurately and ingeniously.

So there is excellent authority for assuming that troweling is not only a trade but something of an art. Even the grudging admiration of bystanders admits it.

They stop in their strolling to wonder what I'm up to now. "What are you doing?" they inquire. "Building a wall?"

It is obvious that I am building a wall.

"A bit knobby, isn't it?" suggests the sidewalk superintendent. I reply that I like my walls knobby. The bystander suggests that the wall will fall down next winter. I answer that if it does I shall stick it up again. If he continues to make critical and scurrilous comments I slap him down with a ten-inch trowel.

Very pleasant conversation can be picked up by a man building a wall, not too energetically, beside the public highway. This is why I sometimes wonder what roads are for.

My speedster friends insist that a road should be nothing but the shortest distance between two points. They consider a curving highway

My Own Four Walls

a crime, a narrow country lane an insult to civilization. They speak of a smooth stretch of concrete as beautiful, but a dirt road winding lazily through hills and meadows is a hideous mess.

The ancient truth is that a road is not a race track but should play its part in a plan of reasonable living. People should walk and talk on roads, as they did a thousand years before automobiles were made. A road should be a market place, as it was in old Egypt and Babylonia. A road should be a place to play, as a road still is in a sheltered village of Europe.

Once I endeavored to expound this philosophy to Kesniel Acton as we hurtled home from a week end in the Catskill Mountains. "A road," said he, "is something on which you travel from one place to another as quickly as possible."

It wasn't worth further argument, especially as there is an old proverb to the effect that you shouldn't look a gift ride in the speedometer. So we drove frantically and lawfully home, assuming that a few miles above fifty per hour don't count. If there is a law that you mustn't drive less than forty miles an hour, we didn't break that one either. We reached home ten minutes behind the driver's schedule, which almost broke his heart, and then pottered about doing nothing in particular until bedtime. Later I dreamed I was a greyhound running after a mechanical rabbit on a concrete track. When I caught up with the rabbit we sat down and played cribbage. After that the rabbit chased me around the track and turned into a Pennsylvania state policeman.

Our own road is not what it used to be, for which thank goodness. In early deeds covering the property it is spoken of as the Mill Road, usually with the added name of the man who owned the mill. Now it is known as Alden Road, honoring its first modern householder, and the name of Mill Road has mysteriously moved over to what the ancient deeds call the New Road.

When first we lived on Alden Road it was no better than a wide gutter between two hillsides. They shed storm water like a duck's back, and the water ran away with the road. Every spring the road was resurfaced with slag, and the first cloudburst of summer stripped it down to bedrock again. So the borough councilmen at last put their heads together and built a concrete road, with slightly concave sidewalks which also serve as gutters. My own road assessment for the improvement was $700. You may remem-

XVII. Laid on with a Trowel

ber that Ben Yerkes, in 1832, paid $700 for the house, outbuildings and ten acres of land.

The seasonal floods which strive to wash the road away are somewhat worse than they used to be, I suppose, since so many householders have skinned their properties over with cement and macadam. Drainage of surface water has been one of my own particular problems. One year we miscalculated in building a flight of steps, and when warm rain brought a quick thaw at winter's end all the water in the world cascaded down the cellarway and needed to be pumped out by the local fire engine. Under such circumstances a man can be thankful for an old-fashioned cellar with a dirt floor.

Now the watersheds work pretty well, partly because the steps and pavements follow logical lines of traffic. Coming down the road, you may turn off conveniently by a wide flight of steps, cross the lawn, climb more steps to the tea terrace and outdoor fireplace, thence by the rose trellis to more steps which lead away into the woods garden.

It may be that the best fun of an outdoor fireplace is building it. It is also good fun to sit before an outdoor fire in early autumn and slap mosquitoes, though I often wish the fireplace hadn't such a healthy appetite. But to drowse before a glowing evening fire, lulled by the autumnal symphony of crickets and katydids, is a reward for sore muscles and an occasional splash of cement in your eye or back hair.

The fireplace backs up against the vegetable garden, a convenient arrangement for disposing of weeds, brush and cornstalks. It is convenient, too, to hold a picnic beside the fire, snatching sweet corn straight from the stalk into the boiling pot before it can lose the least of its savor. Afterwards you may throw the corncobs and paper plates on the fire.

Arch and chimney of the fireplace are fortified with old iron. A gardener with architectural ideas and intentions should never permit the junkman to rob him of old pipe, bedframes or heavy wire. They will serve for reinforcement as well as the finest iron made for the purpose, a commodity which costs more than it is worth in amateur masonry.

Away from the fireplace curves a low wall supporting the vegetable patch and leading to the rose trellis, located in the garden's sunniest spot. Thence you may wander, if you will, to The Battlements.

The Battlements were named by Leslie Howard. We first met at a tea

My Own Four Walls

party in his honor, in Philadelphia, at which I was nearly the only other male present and helped him on with his coat. "Thank heaven that's over," said he.

I reminded him of it on the liner Berengaria several years later, and he was still thankful it was over. Later he invited me to his lovely home near Dorking, in Surrey, and I wished he might return the visit on his next trip to America. He came here in the fall of 1936 to play *Hamlet* and agreeably remembered the invitation as given and accepted.

So we strolled in the garden, bleak and bare in the bitter cold of November, and inspected a section of the rock garden not yet finished. "I'm thinking of calling this The Battlements," I suggested, "and it seems right and proper that Hamlet should dedicate them."

Mr Howard waved his pipe at them and said, "They're dedicated." An imperishable inscription in cement now records this simple but impressive ceremony.

Main purpose of The Battlements and the rest of the rock garden is to give a home to tulips, daffodils and other bulbs which lay a carpet for the coming spring. They thrive in the stone pockets and are willing to bloom there a dozen years without moving. The reason, perhaps, is that they are thoroughly dried out before winter by plentiful drainage and the hungry roots of the great maples which shadow the house and its nearby garden. Shadow it so much, indeed, that nothing much will grow there in midsummer.

Near The Battlements, but on a lower level reached by winding steps, stands the springhouse. It is absurd to call it a springhouse, for there is no spring in its depths, though in wet weather there will be water there. But it looks like a springhouse. It stands, moss-mildewed and ivy-clad, hard by the house beneath the spotted buttonwood tree. A trumpet vine overhangs its arched roof and clumps of iris crowd around it. Its stones are weather-worn and patched with faint color, unlike the cold gray granite which comes out of quarries.

Experts in antiquity have dated the springhouse as belonging to the late eighteenth century and have mused rather prettily about the patient labor which built it. The inside arch, in particular, is impressively constructed of heavy and shapeless stone and supports the vaulted roof and two feet of earth above it. Hardly anything could be more typical of elementary architecture in Montgomery County, Pennsylvania.

XVII. Laid on with a Trowel

Which is all very well, but the springhouse was built about 1920, mainly because I had a lot of stone lying around and was obliged to build something. Why not a springhouse?

Nowadays I can think of no reasonable excuse for building a springhouse in that location, but I am not obliged to please anybody with reasons. For a few years we did keep butter and milk down there, at the bottom of a flight of steps leading twelve feet underground. But now there is nothing down there but a subnormal temperature and spiders.

Yet the springhouse adds an authentic bit of atmospheric architecture to the old farmhouse, which is in most respects so much altered that its own ancestors wouldn't know it. Had I been more thoughtful in this respect I would have preserved the well, for the same reason, which is now lost beneath the laundry. The only way we know the well is still there is that the water from the washing machine drains into it, falling fourteen feet to the bottom with a faint splash.

Now I wish I had the well where I could get some good of it. The well should be out where it could be seen and admired, with a windlass and an old oaken bucket and a stout grating to keep small children from falling into it and fishing in it. If I had the well I wouldn't use the water in it. But I could holler down it.

You must take my word for the well, unless you care to pour a bucket of water on the laundry floor and listen to it arriving at the well's bottom.

A recent addition to the garden's architecture is a lily pool, so far with no flowering lilies in it. But there are goldfish in it. Three goldfish, by the last census, because I have found by experience that young children may ask embarrassing biological questions about two goldfish. They never ask questions about three goldfish.

Sometimes there is also a cat in the lily pool. One lesson a kitten must learn by trial and error is the futility of fishing for goldfish in a lily pool. Two or three generations of kittens have tried plucking a breakfast from the pool. Eventually a kitten falls in and scrambles out again, which probably amuses the goldfish immensely.

In anticipation only, so far, is the tower which will crown and wind up the garden's architectural undertakings. It will be a smallish tower, a one-man tower, with an upper level large enough for an easy chair and

My Own Four Walls

some kind of a cell beneath. Inside the cell could be stored the lawn mower and garden hose. The upper level would be for sitting and thinking.

Adolf Hitler built himself a tower for thinking and sitting, though I don't think much of what he thought up there. That may be the fault of his thinking apparatus or the raw material in his mind. No man can think better than his brain permits, and he can only think of what he has in mind, whether it be put there by reading, experience or bad company.

I don't think Hitler's thinking was any fault of his tower. A tower may be the ideal place for thinking, though if you can't get a tower the top of a mountain will do.

Probably you don't absolutely need a tower to think. Kipling said that "a man's mind is wont to tell him more than Seven Watchmen sitting in a tower." But a tower helps.

XVIII

A Garden of Good Intentions

My godfather in journalism, the late Jay E. House, once wrote the rather savage opinion that "flowers bloomed on the earth two million years ago; men who have quit having fun have been trying to raise them ever since."

I do not agree that men raise flowers only in a feeble and frustrated effort to have fun. Nor is flower gardening a confessional of senile decay and disappointed devilishness. I prefer to believe, with all good gardeners, that it is a good idea and pleasant employment to create a little order in a world of tragic confusion, a little beauty amid so much ugliness. That is the well-meaning gardener's good intention, even though he fail in it.

It was two years after we settled in our antiquated farmstead that we turned attention to its flower garden. Nothing was left of it then except a few peonies, lilies of the valley and clumps of golden glow and a broken picket fence too far gone for repair and strangled in poison ivy. The rest of the place was plain farmyard. The track of the wagon wheel and footprint of the cow were still upon it. Weeds, brambles and nettles flourished mightily, and nothing much else.

The turning point toward better things came when my parents crossed the Atlantic to spend a while with us and heal the heartaches of a war which robbed them of a son, my younger brother. With her my mother brought the understanding love of flowers and an English skill in caring for them. Six months later a few square yards below the house were her particular domain, crowded with bloom and neater than almost any part of the garden has been since then.

My Own Four Walls

The neighbors spoke of it admiringly as a typical English garden. But there is no such thing as an exclusively English garden. There are innumerable small gardens in England, so closely watched and tended that they are full of color and fragrance from early spring until late autumn. But the same sort of garden might be made almost anywhere except in northern Siberia and the Great American Desert. Principal secret of the English cottage gardens is that they are small enough for one gardener's loving care and management. They can be kept alive and happy, if no better tools are to be had, with an ordinary table fork, a pair of scissors and the day's drainings from the icebox. They like a little dishwater, too, if there's not too much soap in it.

Sometimes I still yearn for a small garden in which I might know every flower by name and nature. A large garden easily gets out of hand, like overbold enterprises and ambitions of any kind. And I would sooner share the joys and sorrows of every nasturtium and zinnia in eleven square yards of garden patch than to be casually acquainted with five thousand tulips and two hundred pink geraniums.

Somewhere there lies a happy mean between the too-tiny garden and the oversized estate, and I am still seeking it. In the hopeful flush of every fresh springtime the garden is always overreaching itself, but by October I am resolved to be satisfied next season with smaller and better flower beds and borders.

I have no envy, certainly, of those horticultural royalists who never discover how sharper than a serpent's tooth it is to have a cutworm nibbling the roots of your antirrhinums. They walk briefly in their splendid gardens when they happen to think of it, hire and fire three gardeners twice a month and go away somewhere else for a vacation when the blossoms of midsummer reach their greatest glory. They are welcome to their simple and expensive pleasures. But they are denied the satisfaction of groveling in the dirt with fork and trowel, the reward of raising a sensitive salpiglossis or bashful lobelia, the thrill of the battle with the beetle and all the peaceful pleasures of the watering can.

Nor are they members in good standing of the great brotherhood of gentlemen gardeners, an international fraternity bound in friendship by mutual sympathies and understanding, who speak their own language, practice a communal charity and recognize their own code of etiquette.

XVIII. A Garden of Good Intentions

It is correct, for example, to admire your friend's seedling asters and aquilegias though they may look like weeds in an abandoned brickyard. In return your friend is required to pay a visit someday and admire your seedlings. Good gardeners will exchange gifts, such as cuttings of Sweet William or clumps of iris, but must not inquire what happened to them when they call again. No gardener may say to another that the place looks poorly now, "but you should have seen it a week ago." It is tacitly agreed among gardeners that the garden never looks as well today as it did last week or will next week. Especially next week, since gardeners live by the hope that springs eternal amid the poison ivy of experience.

A garden-minded visitor, moreover, must share his host's imaginative enthusiasms for what the place will look like when it is finished, which means never. After which both may call it a day and see what's in the icebox.

Certain common offenses against the proprieties are recognized by the floricultural code. Not quite respectable are those who bring a restless dog when calling on friends in the country. The poor dog, it is explained, has been shut up in the city all week, which is supposed to excuse the beast for chasing a squirrel or cat through a bed of tulips. Equally out of order is the chap who carries a cane and practices chip shots and putting on your young lawn, and a public menace is the lady who declares she loves cut flowers and plainly expects you to cut your very best for her.

Good garden manners are best displayed in conversation. The visitor's correct attitude is that of expert admiration; the host must murmur, with Shakespeare, "a poor thing, but mine own." Both know by experience how far short a garden falls of the good intentions of the man who makes it. Both know that the other dreams, even now, of next season's taller tulips and prettier petunias.

It is this constant eye on a hopeful future which justifies the gardener and all his works. The outer world in which we live has become hideous with instant necessities which crowd out all cheerful thought for the morrow. Daily we read and hear that the outlook, at best, is bleak, dark, dangerous and calamitous. So it becomes symbolic that the good gardener, though empires totter and civilization shakes in its shoes, goes ahead with his chores in hope and faith that all may yet be well. He never doubts that spring will come again though there are only forty-six shopping days till

My Own Four Walls

Christmas and a wintry wind rattles the bare bones of his garden. And so he tucks away tulips in the cold and clammy soil and knows they will be beautiful next April, though now they look like uninteresting onions.

In a garden shaded heavily by old maple trees, as ours is, the bulbs of spring have an important part to play. They will obligingly be in bloom before the shadow falls across their living room. So there are more bulbs in the garden than I can count or remember exactly where I put them.

There is no order to their arrangement. I prefer a garden of mixed and scrambled tulips. I like to let them wander about the place and enjoy themselves. It seems that tulips must be unhappy when planted in ranks and battalions like soldiers on dress parade. So should daffodils turn up here and there as though by happy accident, and it is absurd to say that sixty hyacinths together are better than half a dozen.

More difficult to defend is the opinion that color arrangements need not be too carefully considered. Yet by hit-and-miss planting in late autumn the gardener may merit many surprises in spring, when some combinations turn out very well and none too badly.

But there are infinite opportunities for differences of opinion in gardening. The reason is hinted in a verse of doubtful authorship, concerning a gentleman who seems to have no other claim to fame.

> *A little garden Little Jowett made,*
> *And fenced it with a little palisade;*
> *If you would know the mind of Little Jowett,*
> *This little garden don't a little show it.*

I hope this garden of mine does not too closely pattern after the mind of the man who made it. Yet in some respects it does. It reflects a curious and inexplicable interest in architecture. It is illogical and irregular and doesn't stay put for two seasons in succession. And it is manifestly unfinished, as I am.

Perhaps I don't want to finish it. If ever I finish it I'll have nothing to do but sit in it until I grow roots. I do sit in it some, of course, but mainly to consider what's next to be done. There are several uncompleted areas concerning which I am still awaiting light and leading. In the meantime visitors must take my word for it or look the other way.

The rambling rock garden is typical. It is not a true rock garden, for

XVIII. A Garden of Good Intentions

real rock plants demand a hot and scathing sun, and this is merely a terraced affair at the foot of the tall maples, full of bulbs in the spring and mostly pachysandra for the rest of the year. It has taken a dozen years to develop, and the job isn't finished. Three men and a piece of machinery could have built the whole works in a week. But I did it myself, a little at a time, and don't have to share the pride and credit of it with a concrete mixer.

What's the frightful hurry, anyway? There is overmuch anxiety in the modern world to get things done, though all philosophers agree that the greatest joy lies in the doing of them. There is too much bragging about rapid transit, and nobody sings the praises of slow motion. But you may take your car along the highway at seventy miles an hour and I'll take a walk along a country lane, and we shall see who gets the best of it. It was Kahlil Gilbran, whoever he may have been, who pointed out that "turtles can tell more about the road than hares."

This flower gardening should be an easygoing hobby, not a grim and serious business. It is the dictionary's definition that a hobby is "that which a person persistently pursues or dwells upon with zeal or delight, as if riding a horse." That all depends, I should say, upon the horse and the equestrian abilities of the person who pursues or dwells upon the horse, and I would be willing to argue that the dictionary is wrong anyway. But I am certain that no hobby should be a taskmaster, but rather an agreeable traveling companion on life's long highway.

It is also a matter of principle that no man should work too hard at his hobby. Who was it said that whatever is worth doing is worth doing well? He was talking for effect, and the truth was not in him. Some things should be done not too well, or somebody else should be hired to do them properly. I could take up knitting and in six months of arduous effort and practice might learn to knit a sweater almost as well as a machine might do it. But it would be better to knit a sweater not too expertly and for the fun of it. Then there would be no doubt that it was a genuine handmade, self-help sweater, fashioned with my own fingers. "See that sweater," admiring friends would exclaim. "He made it himself. The boy's clever, but not too clever."

No matter how real and earnest his vernal ambitions may be, a gardener's good intentions go to seed in the summer's first heat wave. By

My Own Four Walls

mid–August, indeed, I am convinced that we were meant to be lazy creatures, only working to keep ourselves warm. And when the garden falls to pieces under the first frost I feel sure of it.

Yet in the dead of winter good intentions sprout again, like biennials in the cold frame. They may flower in full glory during a February blizzard, when comes the mid-winter crop of seed catalogs. Out come pencil and paper. Clear the living-room table and shut off that confounded radio, because the man of the house is going gardening.

It was while the wind howled dismally around the rooftree that I laid out last winter one of the finest herbaceous borders of my entire horticultural career. All the old-fashioned favorites were in it, with a splendid showing of Gypsophila Paniculata (see page 47 of the catalog), "a plant possessing a grace not found in any other perennial, forming a symmetrical mass two or three feet in height and covered with minute pure white flowers." The border was edged with Anagallis Grandiflora, "completely covered during the greater part of the season with small but brilliant flowers in an unusual range of colors." At decent intervals I put in patches of

XVIII. *A Garden of Good Intentions*

Dimorphotheca Aurantiaca. "The flowers, which are three inches across, are a unique rich glossy orange gold with dark disk and halo. These glitter in the sunshine and present a magnificent sight when in full bloom."

And no Japanese beetles, of course, or other insect pests. By taking thought I entirely exterminated Japanese beetles from the flowers of fancy in my herbaceous borders.

There were a number of other novelties in my winter garden, but most of it was taken up with hybrid Hosea Waterers, a few double Dreers and Michells and some splendid clumps of Buists and Burpees.

I need hardly argue the superiority of indoor horticulture over the common or garden kind. One grave weakness with the latter is that it must be done in dirt. No ordinary dirt will do, either. Every flower or vegetable worth growing must be planted in a "rich sandy loam" or a "slightly acid humus," which are the kinds of dirt that nobody ever has in his garden. There is an insistent demand, moreover, in all textbooks and treatises on gardening for "well-rotted cow manure." Only the rarest of flowers will fulfill the promise of the catalogs without a liberal diet of well-rotted cow manure. Yet it is notoriously difficult for an average suburbanite, even as you and I, to obtain a well-rotted cow when he succumbs to the consequences of man's first disobedience and resolves to cultivate his garden.

The solution is winter gardening, indoor gardening, abstract, romantic and idealistic gardening. It permits no prowling cutworm to slit the throat of a columbine, no crawling caterpillar to gnaw a rose to rags and tatters. No slugs or snails lurk in its rockeries, no blight corrupts its innocent pansies and primulas. It is the only kind of gardening that knows no disappointments or failures, for in the bright lexicon of Burpee there's no such word as fail.

It is the cleanest kind of gardening, and nobody ever caught a case of hay fever or double pneumonia while doing it. It needs no tools except a pencil and paper and a collection of the imaginative romances called seed catalogs. It is comparatively inexpensive. And it serves nicely to keep a man out of mischief during the long hard winter and the spring-fever season, which is about the best argument that can be offered for any kind of gardening.

A winter garden is a garden of good intentions, and so is every little garden that was ever planted and cared for. For the plain and perpetual fact of all flower gardening is that it falls short forever of the gardener's dream. The roses do not live up to their advance notices. The ruffled petunias sprout thick in the seed flats and die of chicken pox and measles in early infancy. The color pattern of the perennial border is spoiled by seedling phlox that has reverted to type and a painful purple. The asters grow moldy with blight and there are nasty insects on the nasturtiums.

But the good intentions of gardening are worth their price in its disappointments. It is an outrageous untruth and invention of the devil, moreover, to say that the highway to hell is paved with good intentions. More likely it isn't paved at all, but is a slippery toboggan slide on which men of good intentions must fight for a foothold and clutch at straws as they climb out of the pit their ancestors digged for them.

My own theory is that inventions, not intentions, pave the road to personal damnation and disaster for civilization. An amazing amount of human ingenuity has been dedicated to the making of machines which have turned out to be more trouble and torment than they are worth. The list might include the lawn mower, a necessary evil of the gardener's equipment. It certainly should include the mechanical marvel and atrocity known as the airplane, designed for ostensibly peaceful purposes and principally used for dropping bombs on the patient craftsmanship of centuries, the little homes and beloved gardens of people who hardly know what this war, or any war, is all about.

It may be the bitterest indictment on our fallen race that civilization seems determined to pave the pathway of progress with good inventions and go to hell on them. Someday it may seem wiser that men should remember the advice of Voltaire and the example of Adam and "cultivate their gardens."

XIX

The Care and Feeding of Carrots

One of the wisest and most respected members of our community is Bishop Alfred Acton, and I think I know one reason why. In our earliest years of matrimony, when we lived next door to the Acton home, I often watched him weeding his way along a row of carrots in his vegetable garden.

The weeding and thinning of carrots cannot be done well with hoe or cultivator. It must be done in the traditional position of piety, down on hands and knees. Each several weed, every superfluous carrot, must be taken from the row by hand. The process is not difficult and need not be tedious. The task takes no thought, so the mind is free to ponder of many things, to plan and meditate.

Weeding carrots never threatened to make a bishop of me but might have made me a poet if I had planted enough carrots. Some of my favorite verses, such as they are, came of this supremely reflective employment.

Everybody who has bought a bunch of carrots knows that the amateur cannot possibly raise carrots at a profit. So there must be some other reason for raising them. It may be that the great gain of raising and caring for carrots is what you think about while working on them and sometimes the fact that you can work on them without thinking at all. The same goes, in varying degree, for almost everything else done and raised in a vegetable garden.

A small truck patch should not be considered an investment, its output to be measured by ordinary yardsticks of profit and loss. This I learned, once and for all, by keeping careful books one summer on the vegetable

My Own Four Walls

garden. Favoring the fruits of my toil as much as possible and crediting them in the ledger at top prices of the local huckster, I came out none too well in the final reckoning. By incredible industry I cleared about $55 over the costs of seeds, tools and fertilizer, which is poor pay for half a year's work. My fresh vegetables paid me nine cents an hour for my labor, and there are easier ways to make that much money.

There are better reasons for raising your own vegetables. One is that a vegetable garden is something to do at small cost. Before the dogs of war broke loose the civilized world was finding itself with a lot of spare time on its hands and no clear idea what to do with it. H.G. Wells saw it coming more than twenty years ago, when he promised that someday "natural power harnessed in machines will be the general drudge. What drudgery is inevitable will be done as a service and duty for a few years or months out of each life."

This was agreeable prophecy, though a little vague around the edges. But Mr Wells forgot to tell us what should be done with spare time when it wasn't needed for work.

Some spare time can be spent in reading the works of H. G. Wells, but not three or four days a week. The problem of this surplus of leisure was just beginning to worry the world when the bottom fell out of everything, back in 1929, and made matters worse. During the Depression it was discovered that spare time can be a nuisance and a bore if you have no spare money to spend in it. Most modern amusements are expensive, and many modern people have lost the art of amusing themselves in pleasant but unprofitable occupations.

The care of a carrot bed is the symbolic solution. It takes up far more time than it is worth, but the time is agreeably spent. And the thinning and weeding of carrots, moreover, is one minor drudgery which Mr Wells and his machinery are very unlikely to take over.

So I defend my vegetable garden not as an offset to the high cost of living but for the spiritual peace and profit to be gained from it. It proved its worth in 1925, when I suddenly and painfully lost my job as a teacher. What to do? The thing to do was to take three months off and dig a garden as though everything in the world depended on it. At the end of the summer I had a few bushels of beans and potatoes and an idea what to do next and how to go about it.

XIX. The Care and Feeding of Carrots

I gained something more by those weeks of sweat and labor in the truck patch. They healed the sore places on my self-respect and vanity. And when I dug the potatoes, finally, I wasn't mad any more at anybody.

What a solitary struggle with a garden can do for you was well phrased by Robert Frost, the poet. "The real thing you do is the lonely thing." You can have it out with yourself while swinging a long-handled shovel, my favorite garden weapon, and take a few comforting wallops at your imagined ills and enemies, represented by a stubborn clod of clay or sod of grass roots.

Actually there was more whacking done at a thicket of blackberry canes running wild where I wanted the vegetables to be. This was once a magnificent blackberry patch and has yielded more than two hundred quarts of berries in a season, from the sale of which the youngsters derived their vacation pocket money. But all that was before the Japanese beetles came like a devastating cloud of locusts and sat down on the blackberry patch. Not satisfied to gorge their loathsome appetites with berries, leaving a mere handful for me, they must further wipe their feet on every berry in the patch and blight its hopes of ripening. So regretfully, at last, blackberries gave way to beans and corn, beets and carrots, peas and potatoes.

Some other fruit in the old farm garden still lives there. There is an ancient apple tree and a no-account pear. Both are mountains of bloom in spring and no good to anybody at harvest time. They can stay where they are, for I can always buy apples but not the company of a crooked tree in bloom.

I have tried to raise peaches and coddled a few trees to yield one fair crop. But peach trees die too young, long before the prime of life, probably from arboreal croup, whooping cough and other infantile ailments. I gave up grapes when the beetles came. I have one good cherry tree, and the birds get up earlier than I do and eat the cherries. Half a dozen respectable apple trees are now beginning to bear, but take up too much room for the rent they pay.

So my strictly agricultural ambitions are now concentrated on vegetables. Their serried ranks, in mid-summer, make a good showing, though I know full well that the family could eat the whole works down to the ground in a dozen sittings. It would take twenty closely cultivated acres,

My Own Four Walls

I suppose, to feed the whole tribe, and my morning basket of beans, carrots and tomatoes is not much more than a gesture.

Yet the stuff is good, and a wise gardener will prefer to plant such vegetables as are infinitely better when fresh-picked and quickly cooked. Sweet corn and Limas, of course, and tomatoes allowed to ripen on the vine. He will pull his carrots when they are half grown and fit for human beings to eat, not merely rabbits. And in the smallest radish he will take satisfaction that no money can buy from the huckster or chain store.

Few of my vegetables would be worth showing at a county fair. Some are pitifully small, as was the most recent crop of cucumbers. I am through with cucumbers, in fact, since I gathered my crop and one of the youngsters wanted a cucumber with which to make a sandwich. "Daddy has a cucumber in the refrigerator," said Sylvia. "If you can't find it, look for a pickle."

It is admitted that nobody around the house admires my vegetables as much as I do. I regard them as really beautiful. Vegetables are beautiful, as still-life painters found out a long time ago. But it is a little unusual when a prose writer in the public press cuts loose in a kind of ecstasy in praise of vegetables, not for their nutritive values but for the loveliness of their line and color.

The lady who did so was named Clementine Paddleford, writing for the women's pages of the New York *Herald Tribune*. Miss Paddleford went to market and came home with half a bushel of fresh-picked adjectives and all the colors of the rainbow. "Pale green comes the fresh sage, bush green the thyme. Sunset hues show up in the rhubarb. Huckleberries and dewberries add blues and blacks to the market spectrum. See the saffrons and chromes of the cantaloupes, the purple-tipped asparagus and the pale leeks, their thready roots like witch's hair."

Nice going, Miss Paddleford, and you might also mention the creamy white of the cauliflower, the passionate scarlet of the radish and tomato, the gay yellow of the carrot and the somber green of the curly kale.

Hard work made this garden grow, plus some help, in season, from the stable where dwells my father-in-law's horse. The forgotten rule of most people's vegetable gardening is that you must put something into the soil if you want to get much out of it. Some of it is fertilizer and the rest hard labor.

XIX. The Care and Feeding of Carrots

By nature the soil of my garden is heavy, thick with clay, and needs all the humus and ashes it can get. More still it needs digging, which is one reason why I discover every April that there are approximately eight hundred muscles in the human anatomy, most of them susceptible to horticultural exercise.

I have no respect for exercise as such, agreeing with the political hero of my English childhood, Joseph Chamberlain, that "any man who has walked downstairs and upstairs in the same day has had enough exercise for a gentleman." And with Martial, the old Roman, who wanted to know "Why do strong arms fatigue themselves with frivolous dumbbells?" Martial meant the things you swing in matutinal setting-up exercises, not on the dance floor, but the sentiment is sound for both. Exercise should serve some useful purpose, or there is small sense in taking it.

There is plenty of it to be had in the planting and care of a vegetable garden, and the most ingenious expert in physical culture could not devise such various gymnastics, bendings, stretchings and strainings as are involved in the cultivation of carrots. Their sufficient reward, aside from the carrots, is a pleasing sense of weariness and well-being and sometimes a few pangs of lumbago.

Lumbago is a mysterious ailment, and nobody seems to know why one man gets it by lifting an oversized rock and another by sitting in the draft of an electric fan. It is also one of the most monopolizing of the natural shocks which flesh is heir to. Nothing else matters much to a man with a crick and misery in the small of his back. Nations may fall and institutions totter, but few things concern him seriously except the problem of sitting down and the equally painful problem of getting up again.

But there is nothing like lumbago, either, to arouse the helpful instincts of neighborly humanity. Nearly everybody has had lumbago, and everybody knows a cure for it. If a lawyer pleading his case before the Supreme Court of the United States should suddenly cry out from a poignant pang of lumbago, the nine wise men on the bench would each hand down a different decision what to do about it, allowing the Constitution and the case before the Court to wait their turn. This is a friendly world, after all, and lumbago does much to make it so.

All these may be trifling arguments for laboring with the spading fork and hoe, but bigger reasons would not be better ones. Chief of them all,

My Own Four Walls

perhaps, are the peace in the present and confidence in the future that come of vegetable gardening. For it takes us back to the land and the knowledge that wealth, whether little or large, comes first from the land and man's labor on it.

This may be hard doctrine for some folk. Your capitalist, stockbroker or traveling salesman believes he makes money by selling something for more than he paid for it, whether it be merchandise or securities or human labor. Perhaps he makes money, but not wealth. As I weed my way along the carrot row I am compelled to believe that all real wealth must somehow be extracted out of the raw materials of which this world is made. It may be gold, oil, metal or merely carrots. But the land and human labor on the land must still be the essential foundations of human society and all its prosperity.

Ben Yerkes made his wealth that way even though he was a wheelwright more than a farmer. My house was built that way, not with the profits on a quick turn in Wall Street. And those who lived here before me, I think, suffered less from the slings and arrows of outrageous fortune than those who now own their land, sliced up into small pieces and called real estate. They had no great wealth, but they lived close to the land from which it came.

Today few of us can own enough land to support us in the style to which we would like to be accustomed. But a certain spiritual support and stability still come of land ownership if only the owner will do something else with the land but walk on it. It may help to steady him through economic upheavals and crises which are nothing new under the sun but seem more painful than they used to be.

I remember the kitchen gardens of my kinfolk in the West Country of England. They worked by day in the mill or shoe factory and were home in time for a long twilight with garden tools. Their gardens were the width of their little houses and stretched as far back as a lenient landlord would let them go. That was forty years ago, but in 1931 I was back there for a brief and unexpected visit, together with others from faraway America.

After the third cup of tea it was suggested that we must inspect the garden and admire the magnificence of the potatoes and the promise of the Brussels sprouts. There were pigs to see, too, exactly as there were

XIX. The Care and Feeding of Carrots

forty years ago, though not precisely the same pigs. But it was the same garden.

The man who kept it so long may not have had much fun by today's restless reckoning, but he was still alive and able-bodied and not aware that he had missed much. He had lived through two or three depressions without complaining much or losing much. He never had much to lose.

What he had forty years ago was a garden, and in 1931 he still had it.

XX

The Gentleman Farmer

Now our house is crowded a little too closely by neighbors for complete comfort, but when we acquired it in 1918 there were only three others within half a mile. Across the way lived Winfred Hyatt, but in 1918 he wasn't there. He and his wife were taking holiday in Europe and their home was rented to Oswald Asplundh. And Oswald was keeping chickens in my chicken house.

It was only recently my chicken house and I did not know much about chickens. Otherwise I might not have agreed, when the Hyatts returned and the Asplundhs moved elsewhere, to play caretaker to Oswald's flock until he found another place to put it. It was agreed that it should be done on something like a business basis. I would feed and care for the chickens and could have the eggs and help myself to a chicken dinner every two weeks for my trouble.

As summer drifted into autumn and winter and Oswald didn't come back for his chickens I began to have grave doubts of my bargain. A five-pound fowl every two weeks is poor pay for morning and evening exercises with a flock of hungry hens. Value of their eggs came nowhere near the price of their feed. Cleaning a chicken house is worth $25, I should say, and if you don't clean it the chickens die of numerous and distressing diseases. And when winter came there were no eggs, a great many rats and additional difficulties of heating drinking water and shoveling snow from the chicken yard.

In early spring of our second year of residence Oswald came back and cheerfully asked for his surviving chickens. By that time there were no chickens. I endeavored to convince him that a chicken in the pot every two weeks for ten months means serious depreciation to an original flock

XX. The Gentleman Farmer

of twenty. I could also have showed him receipted bills for fancy feed, charcoal and oystershell which would have cured him of wanting his chickens. But he went away feeling swindled and may still feel so.

I should have known by then that chickens are no good unless they can scratch for half their living at a farmhouse kitchen door. But I owned a large and well-built chicken house and felt bound to use it. In the optimistic mood of April I decided to raise chickens of my own.

Later I realized that I would have saved time and money by buying cold-storage eggs and setting the cat on them, but in my hopeful ignorance I purchased two dozen baby chicks and went after experience with live bait. I carried them home from the city in a perforated suitcase, and all survived the trip except one little fellow who grieved overmuch for his incubator and passed away before we reached city limits. The other twenty-three I put in a washtub beside a hot-water radiator, providing them generously with shells and sand and worms and garden seeds and all the other things that chickens eat and scrupulously shielding them from drafts, the children and the household cat.

They immediately started to peep and peeped continually, day and night, for nearly two weeks. I could never be sure why they peeped, but supposed they were too hot or too cold and adjusted the temperature of the house up and down until most of the family had chronic catarrh.

Finally the peeping diminished, partly because the cat got into the washtub and scrambled six chickens beyond repair. The remnant was transferred to the back of the stove for safer keeping, and the next time the Lady of the House baked a batch of biscuits she cooked four of them.

The others were moved outdoors into a charming little coop which I personally prepared for them. All went well for a week, but then a storm came up in the night and none of the chickens knew enough to come in out of the wet, preferring to crouch by the outer wire and pray for better weather. Three drowned in their tracks. The others I brought into the house and wiped them dry and fed them hot soup and port wine from a medicine dropper, in spite of which two took double pneumonia and died reproaching me.

Eight still remained, and fine young chickens they were, with appetites like ostriches and an infinite capacity for flying out of anything they were put into. One flew into a five-ton truck and another committed

My Own Four Walls

suicide by entering into pointless argument about the cancellation of war debts with an English sheep dog. Four others surrendered unconditionally to the pip, gapes, staggers and foot-and-mouth disease.

Of the remaining pair we expected much and counted our eggs long before they were laid. But it turned out that our two hens were roosters, with no more than a sentimental interest in eggs. I sold one to a neighbor for breeding purposes and the neighbor never paid for it. The lone survivor stayed on awhile, earmarked for a Thanksgiving dinner, and then disappeared overnight. The door of the chicken house was open next morning, but I doubt the rooster opened it.

Any misguided ambitions to raise chickens were finished by now. But there still stood the chicken house. This was in 1920, and I was narrowly on the point of pulling down the chicken house when somebody pointed to the fact that this was no ordinary chicken house. It was a frame building in the strict sense of the phrase. Its main timbers were six inches thick, hand hewn from oak logs. It would be a shocking shame to tear it down for firewood if any better purpose could be found for it.

By this time my English parents were living with us, which was good company but something of a crowd. In early 1921, therefore, I resolved not to tear down the chicken house but to rebuild it. I would make of it a comfortable little cabin for the old folks.

This sort of thing has happened several times when I have wondered what to do with an outbuilding of the old farm which no longer served its appointed purposes. I made no serious mistake by rebuilding the chicken house. The loose and rotted lumber was ripped away and new walls, roof and floor built into the frame. A long living room was added, with a stone fireplace and chimney. I made a small mistake while building the chimney, allowing too little leeway for the flue, which accounts for a curious offset in the outside wall about five feet from the ground. It may look queer but makes no difference to the chimney draft.

Now the chicken house is called Come-Again Cabin, and no cottage was ever more curiously built. For a while its walls and roof were of boards and heavy tar paper. Later I lathed and plastered the walls and shingled the roof. It was several more years before the outside plaster got its second coat and the inside walls were paneled with composition board.

Second year after my parents moved in there was added a room in

XX. The Gentleman Farmer

which my mother could keep her potted plants during the winter. No true Englishwoman can struggle through a winter without potted plants. After the old folks went back to England we somehow inserted a small cellar beneath the house and a pipeless furnace. Later a mechanically minded tenant, Charlie Kintner, worked out part of his rent by installing hot-water heating.

Roughly speaking, Come-Again Cabin was built backwards and upside down. I doubt many other houses ever had cellars shoved beneath them after they were finished and occupied. At any time, even now, additions and alterations may enlarge or improve the place.

All this has been done with utmost concern for economy. The two chimney pots on the cabin came from country sales. Bricks of the terrace are secondhand bricks; the bathtub came from a building wrecker's yard. Much of the building I have done myself, with assistance from able-bodied sons. Tenants have contributed their share.

This is one way to build a house, and the only time I regret it is when making out my income-tax return. In this ridiculous document there is a section requiring me to report rents and royalties, less deductible expenses for maintenance, repairs and depreciation. Depreciation must be based on the character and original cost of the rented property.

I defy the secretary of the treasury, the Department of Internal Revenue and seven certified public accountants to say what Come-Again Cabin cost, what it is worth and how much I may lawfully deduct for its depreciation. What was the land worth, on which it stands, when it was a foul and unprofitable chicken yard? What were the remnants of the chicken house worth? What am I allowed for two chimney pots, picked up for ten cents apiece at country sales? What may I charge for my own labors with hammer and saw, trowel and whitewash brush? What is a chimney worth which cost me $3.00 for cement, nothing for stone and a week's hard labor? What is my electric wiring worth, an amateur job but still in service after twenty years?

Not even in terms of rental can I guess what the place is worth. It rents for relatively little, which is one reason why it has rarely been without a satisfied tenant. In unoccupied intervals it has been useful as a maternity ward, and three of the youngsters were born there, with mother in sight of home but out of hearing of its racket.

My Own Four Walls

Mostly young people and honeymoon couples have lived there, and I have lost count of them. Nor can I remember how many babies have been born there. Mostly my tenants have moved on, when their earnings allowed, to larger quarters or homes of their own. There are always others who want the place.

There may be a moral here for those who worry about the American housing problem. The need is for small houses that do not cost too much for rental. It is not the smallness of them that is desirable, but the low rental. Most small houses, designed for the needs of young people beginning the battle of married life, are built to look like big houses on a small scale and cost three times too much.

This one is not a great deal better than a shack, but in the rosy light of love's young dream a shack may be a palace in fairyland. Even in this more practical and realistic world a rental of $25 per month, including electricity and water, may permit a young couple to put something away for a rainy day and the down payment on a forty-foot lot and an FHA mortgage.

In somewhat the same fashion, though not so thriftily, Ben Yerkes' old wheelwright's shop became a six-room house. It was also called, within the memory of man, the slaughterhouse and may once have been used before as a residence. There was a wide-throated fireplace in what is now the living room, where the unhewn logs supporting the second floor still show. Walls of the original building are twenty inches thick, which permits fine window sills and holds out the heat of summer.

By way of the chicken house and wheelwright's shop I worked up to the barn. That was in 1926, which you may remember was a bad year for building. Everything used in building, in 1926 and 1927, cost twice or three times what it was worth.

But that was at the height of a boom, and a boom is a period in which Americans don't give a hoot what anything is really worth, so long as they can pay its price. It is a suicidal frame of mind, and had something to do with the collapse that came later. It led many of us into wanton extravagance, with the penalty of paying for it when the tide was no longer going our way.

What was left of the barn in 1926 was a crumbling square of stone and the land on which it stood. It was annoying the neighbors by hiding

XX. The Gentleman Farmer

the sunset and breeding rats and spiders. Children fell off its walls occasionally and broke themselves in divers places. Perhaps I should have torn it down for the tons of stone in it. Instead I signed away my life, liberty and pursuit of happiness for something like $8500 and had the barn built into a two-story apartment house. Since the Depression was not yet in sight the building association and bank were willing to finance the job. Three years later they wouldn't lend thirty cents to finance a peanut stand.

The apartment house has worked out fairly well, though its rents are not what they were in 1927. By favor of the slope of the farmyard, each is a first-floor apartment with space for a garden. Fortunately the place was well built, as well as expensively. It should last a long time to come. If you can wait, this is the only sensible and economical way to build anything which you hope to take a profit from. The English have found it out, building their municipal housing projects to stand for sixty years, at least, while too many American houses of modern construction will be lucky to outlast their mortgages.

There are times when I wonder whether it would have been wiser to restore the barn itself rather than rebuild its walls into an apartment house. Now and then I feel the nostalgic need for a barn as I walk around the place in the footsteps of Ben Yerkes and Christian Snyder, who once kept cows and pigs and chickens where my tenants now get their milk, eggs and bacon from an electric refrigerator.

It would be a dim and cavernous barn, sweet-scented with hay on which children could slide and with cross timbers for them to climb. Charles Morrison, who is my editor in chief on the *Public Ledger*, has the barn I want on his farm at Traymore, Pa. Swallows flit in its shadows and cats stalk its floors. Its horses are friendly, its cows phlegmatic, its pigs astonishingly clean and companionable. It houses tons of potatoes and bushels of apples in season. A gentleman farmer would make a morning and evening ritual of visiting such a barn and exchanging compliments with his livestock.

More profitable, perhaps, would be to rebuild the barn for some little-theater group with no home of its own. Lately these stage-struck societies have multiplied amazingly, and there are not enough barns to go round.

But when I find myself regretting the barn I sternly remind myself that a barn without cows is no barn at all and that I am totally unfitted by temperament and experience to care for cows. Cows have calves at inconvenient times of day and night. Cows get up too early in the morning and will not wait for milking until a gentleman farmer has had breakfast. And with all my liking for the ancient handicrafts, I have no appetite at all for milking a cow.

Most overcivilized people have no taste for milking a cow. Many have never watched the milking of a cow, though dimly aware that there is such a process. Most young women don't want to watch the milking of a cow. I don't mind watching it myself, but prefer first to cultivate the cow's acquaintance and be sure that she doesn't care.

There is not so much prejudice against a chicken laying an egg, though I have met one young lady who insisted that science should find some way of laying eggs by machinery. But it is clear that cit6folk, to an almost alarming degree, have refined themselves far away from the farmyard and its employments, exactly as they would wish to hold their noses while passing by a busy barn. It doesn't matter that most of their ancestors kept pigs, milked cows and were forever falling over ducks and chickens at the kitchen door. Those, they seem to think, were days of barbarism, while it is a highly civilized accomplishment to cross the street to the corner store and buy a dozen eggs, a small picnic ham, a stewing chicken and a bottle of Grade A milk.

I share some of these prejudices, so my yearning for a barn is a passing mood. So is the thought that it would be nice to own a springhouse with deep water in which to keep milk bottles and butter crocks. And a well of cool water with an old oaken bucket. For I have carried water from the well in my time, and it's not much fun after the third bucket.

What I would really like on my farm, or what is left of it, is a hydraulic ram. The hydraulic ram is a primitive but thoroughly satisfactory device for making water run uphill under its own power. You need a small and steady stream to make it work, but while the water runs it will work forever.

I can imagine nothing more soothing to the nerves of the weary farmer than to hear the solemn snorting of his hydraulic ram in the silent watches of the night. And if I had one, I could have no end of fun figuring out how a hydraulic ram works. I've been told a dozen times and I still don't know.

XXI

Confessions of a Fundamentalist

Already I have admitted some doubt concerning the alleged labor-saving devices of modern civilization and grave suspicion of its more elaborate inventions. My prejudice may not be a matter of sensible conviction. More likely it comes of a congenital frame of mind.

Probably I am, at heart and core, an old-fashioned fundamentalist. Not in the sectarian sense of the word but in preference for older ways of living and doing things until newer ones have proved their worth beyond question.

For example, ours is a fundamentalist household because we still use ice while nearly all the neighbors have electric refrigerators. I shall not argue whether a leg of lamb and six pounds of butter keep as well in company with a 50-pound cake of ice as in a white enameled cabinet. They keep well enough. So the old-time refrigeration is good enough for me.

This does not say that I am ignorant of these new-fangled conveniences. I have tried most of them, and most of them too soon. We owned the first electric dishwasher in the vicinity, mainly because I was in the electrical-appliance business at the time and could get it at an enormous discount. It was a wonderful machine when it worked, and when it didn't it threw forks and spoons through plates and teacups and wrecked half our chinaware. Since then these deficiencies have been eliminated from electric dishwashers. I still wonder whether they are worth their price and upkeep.

It is the old house itself, perhaps, which persuades me that all the problems of light housekeeping cannot be solved by connecting the home

My Own Four Walls

with an electric light and power plant and pushing a button. There will still be some annoying perplexities left when electricity has had its last word.

In that labor-saving age, I suppose, I shall return home in late evening and be met at the door by a beam of black light which will switch on the lamp in the parlor, notify the folks that the man of the house is home and prepare a fried-egg sandwich and a glass of milk for a late supper. The door will open automatically, recognizing with forty watts of electrical discrimination that this is the master of the house and not a thief in the night. A robot in the living room will remark, "Good evening, sir," and the clock will strike twenty-six minutes past midnight.

As I retire for the night an electric valet will pick up my trousers and take them away to be cleaned and pressed before morning. The bed will be mildly irradiated with ultraviolet light, so that I shall be nicely tanned by 9:30 a.m., at which time a television radio will touch me gently on the shoulder and tell me the news of the day. The bath will be waiting at a temperature regulated by thermostatic control, and a watchful X ray in the kitchen will see to it that the eggs are cooked precisely as I prefer them.

This hints, to my thinking, of a rather terrifying tomorrow, when civilization and all its works will hang by a thread of Number 3 copper wire. In some degree it does so now. It requires, at last count, nine motors and twenty-seven fuses to run my modest rural household. It would be ten motors, except that I stand out stoutly and stubbornly for the old-fashioned safety razor and refuse to electrocute my whiskers with a portable lawn mower. But this is a last and probably futile stand against a rising tide of voltage and amperage which will eventually electrify the least of our habits and occupations.

I have tried to tell the youngsters that it was not always thus. But they don't and won't believe it. Electricity is a part of their lives, like breakfast and brushing their teeth and breaking the windows. They regard it as silly that there should ever have been a time when electricity wasn't discovered.

I have tried to tell them about the old parlor lamp with the green-and-white shade. And the can of coal oil with a potato on the spout. The oil always ran out, you remember, on a particularly vile evening, and you

XXI. Confessions of a Fundamentalist

could walk a mile to the crossroads store for more. If you were thrifty folk you kept a barrel of coal oil in the back yard, and it's a wonder you didn't set the house afire. Sometimes you did.

There was one thing in favor of an old-fashioned oil lamp. On a cold winter's night it warmed the room like a stove. It did the same in summer, too, and could burn up half a pint of moths and beetles in its chimney before bedtime. In those days you lit a lantern to fix the furnace and went to bed with a candle. It's a wonder we lived to tell the tale. There was the time, for instance, when the lamp began to blaze like nobody's business on the dining-room table. Nothing to do about it but open the window and toss the whole works into the garden.

There was gas, of course, but it was expensive stuff, and its light was too far away from where you needed it. You remember the gas mantle and Father putting a match to a new one before lighting the gas. And the lights beginning to burn low and not another quarter in the house to buy more. The way that meter could gobble up quarters in dull and wintry weather!

Those were the good old days. Not so good, though, when it came time to clean the lamp chimneys or put in a new wick. The switch and socket are simpler. They are too darned simple, in fact, which is one reason why there are sixteen lights burning for nobody's benefit when I get home late and everybody else has gone to bed. I swear about it, sometimes, and turn them off. Perhaps I would swear more if I tried to turn on the electric light and there wasn't any.

We discover our dependency on the dynamo and transformer, sometimes, when wind or sleet storms break a wire between the house and power plant. For some years no tree of mine has been responsible for such a disaster. This is because, after a great limb of maple had dropped through part of the roof and the front porch, I took out wind insurance against such accidents. It is testimony to the efficiency of American business that nothing of the sort has happened since.

When a wire does break, due to wind and weather which pass by my insured homestead, the plight of our overcivilized community is pitiable. Clocks stop, oil burners stop, vacuum cleaners and washers stop. A young lady drying her hair with an electric blower is left helpless and bedraggled. The lights go out, but somebody suggests that we listen quietly to the radio until they come on again. The radio is silent. Somebody suggests we

My Own Four Walls

go to the movies, but it is doubtful whether the movies are working either. Everybody looks for a candle and nobody can find one. There remains nothing to do but go quietly and humbly to bed, hoping that daylight will be working as usual tomorrow morning.

All this is symbolic of a score of ways in which the people of the modern world have become too mutually dependent for their own good. And I am constantly reminded, while working and playing around my old farmhouse, that its former inhabitants were not nearly so much at the mercy of machinery or tied to remote and impersonal public utilities by miles of pipe and wire.

Then a man's house was literally his castle, though not a very comfortable one. It is my impression that castles never were comfortable. But they were designed and equipped to hold out against hard weather, the tides of economic disaster and even the tax collector and the plundering bandit, now thinly disguised in the habiliments of polite society and selling brushes, vanilla extract and aluminum ware at the front door.

The important criticism against the ways and customs of those times and peoples is that their battle for life, liberty and the pursuit of happiness took up all their time. They had no leisure. I am sure my adopted ancestors, the early inhabitants of my house, had small leisure in the modern meaning of the phrase. Undoubtedly they worked too hard and played too little. They owned no automobiles, radios, ping-pong tables or rumpus rooms in their cellars. They belonged to no bridge or country clubs. Their hobbies, if any, were mainly an exchange of one kind of hard work for another.

Yet part of the penalty of progress is the discovery that leisure time may be something of an embarrassment and almost always an expense. Rather depressing, too, is the determined effort of recent years to invent occupations for the world's new leisure, supposed to be the byproduct of the mechanization of industry and shorter working hours.

Economists are saying that civilization is headed toward a time when a day's pay will be earned by considerably less than a day's work. Man will continue to live by the sweat of his brow, but only between a late breakfast and time for afternoon tea, with a three-day week end in which to recuperate. All this can be easily proved on paper, especially by Stuart Chase, though it is still difficult to find anybody who is actually doing it.

After reading the arguments for a planned program of leisure you

XXI. Confessions of a Fundamentalist

may wonder how you ever managed to survive a Saturday afternoon and idle Sunday without the advice of experts on what to do with them. You may also wonder, as I do, who it is that needs to be told what to do with his spare time. It isn't you, of course, and it can't be me. I believe I could use four hours more of leisure per diem without difficulty if I had them. I could use one deciding what to do with the other three. I could use one of the remainder resting from my labors during the other two. And there's half the new leisure gone and nothing done.

But the experts in these matters warn us that the blue devils of boredom will get us if we don't watch out, or else we shall spend our spare time foolishly because we don't know any better. They insist we must join clubs, collect something, study the arts and sciences and pick ourselves a profitable and improving hobby.

All this anxiety about superabundant leisure is pseudo-scientific nonsense. The remedy for time on your hands is to own your own four walls, a little house in the country, and build and better it, year by year, closer to your heart's desire.

The blight upon our times is that we have become too much enslaved to the clock and calendar. I have learned by experience, long before Professor Albert Einstein said so, that time is always an illusion and sometimes a snare. I learned from one of my teachers in theological school, the late Bishop Dandridge Pendleton, that even eternity is not an interminable amount of time but a happy state of mind and spirit in which time is of no consequence. Time is a convenient device of this world, if not an invention of the devil. It has no reasonable ratio to happiness, to success, to anything that makes life worth living.

This lesson, for what it is worth, may be taught by living in a house so old that it has lost track of time. Or by working at trades and handicrafts that need not be hurried by any necessity of finishing the work in hand. It is this attribute which makes a hobby of what might otherwise be a hardship. It is this, perhaps, which justifies the years so wastefully, yet agreeably, spent on the restoration and reconstruction of Penepac Manor.

We have chosen that name for the old farmstead, having tried some others. The Pemmapacka Creek, also called the Penepac and Pennypack, no longer bounds the land belonging to the old farmhouse. But had the

My Own Four Walls

creek not been there a century ago, the house and its neighboring buildings would not be here now.

These twenty-two years may be called a trifle compared to what has gone before. They are not much in the reckoning of the tall clock which once ticked time away against our living-room wall and is still doing it only half a mile away. It is the ghost of the clock, perhaps, which whispers that I may take my time as I mend my house or tend my garden. It may also have been a wise Indian of the Pemmapacka Valley who is quoted as answering a white man who complained that he had not enough time for all he wished to do. "Well," said the Indian, "you have all the time there is."

The old house needs an old clock to keep it understanding company. There are numerous clocks around the house, but no two of them tell the same time. In emergency the solution is to add up the time they tell and divide by seven. Least congenial of them all, I think, are the electric clocks, though mostly they tell the time of day with painful accuracy.

So far I have sternly refused a place in the house for one of these clocks which look like desk calendars and show no friendly face or hands. It is not enough for me, nor any civilized person, to know that it is now 2:46 exactly. The round face of an old-fashioned clock counts the hours that are gone and the hours to come. It considers not only the fleeting moment but the past and future. That is what a clock is for, not merely to tell the time.

In the transept of Wells Cathedral, eight miles from my birthplace in Somerset, England, hangs the curious clock of Peter Lightfoot, who made it about seven hundred years ago to keep time in Glastonbury Abbey. The original inward parts of the clock are no longer there but are kept in South Kensington Museum, in London, as curiosities of ancient handiwork. Yet they are said to be still in good working order, and Peter Lightfoot's clock is believed to be the world's oldest piece of working mechanism, excepting such simple devices as locks and some quaint instruments of medieval torture.

It seems right and reasonable that the most venerable of machines should be a clock. And if the old grandfather's clock were back in its place against my living-room wall it could sneer at every other machine in a semimechanized household, including vacuum cleaner, washer, can opener

XXI. Confessions of a Fundamentalist

and numerous other comforts and conveniences of light housekeeping in the modern manner. All such inventions are infants compared to a clock. Yet they are called labor-saving and time-saving devices, ignoring the plain testimony of every clock that time cannot be saved but only used and spent.

Nothing else but a clock, either, could leave behind a ghost to haunt a house, as this clock has done. I cannot imagine the ghost of a fireless cooker or waffle iron or even a butter churn or circular saw. Only a clock has human character enough to haunt a house.

Other argument in favor of the frills and furnishings of the modern American household is that they mysteriously represent something called a "standard of living." The American standard of living, in particular, is mainly measured in bathtubs, radios, refrigerators and automobiles, never in true terms of spiritual comfort and happiness.

Well, I must take it for granted that everybody has a standard of living. There must be one in our house if I could locate it. Perhaps it has fallen behind the piano or the kids have been using it for a dart board. Perhaps it's in the pocket of my old working trousers. Perhaps it's in the dictionary.

It is in the dictionary. A standard of living is "an irreducible minimum of economic goods and services which a given community or given class in the community insists on having, and in default of which it will steal or die." That's laying it on rather thick, but I get the general idea. If you can't live without tiled bathrooms you have lost your standard of living. If meat balls for dinner make you miserable, your standard of living is dangerously below par. If you can't have what you think you want, in short, you are a pathetic victim of economic injustice and catastrophe and might as well end it all.

Yet if the dictionary knows what it is talking about, as it usually does, the standard of living is more a state of mind than an economic yardstick. It doesn't concern what you have but what you can philosophically get along without. And by that definition I have no right to think that those who once lived in my house without thermostats, telephones or electric egg beaters were denied any claim to content and happiness.

They must have been optimists in spite of all, or they would never have stuck it out. They must have been philosophers, though Henry

My Own Four Walls

Mencken declares "there is no record in human history of a happy philosopher." More than all they were realists, I imagine, as anybody must be who lives on a farm. And there is no defensible optimism that cannot face realities and make the best of them, even though the best be poor indeed.

I do not wish myself to be a philosopher, though philosophy is the poor man's luxury and the only one, so far, which nobody has tried to put a tax upon. Too many folk wear their philosophies like strait jackets and never have any fun. And too many optimists are imitations of the legendary Sunny Jim, a familiar figure in advertising twenty years ago who hasn't been around much lately. I don't know what happened to Sunny Jim, but perhaps he laughed too loud in the face of reality and dislocated his funny bone. Life may be a mildly amusing affair, but most of it is nothing to crack a rib about.

A fundamentalist is also a realist, a man who makes sure the ship is sinking before he takes to a doubtful raft or life preserver. He sticks to the icebox until he is convinced the electric refrigerator is worth its price and maintenance. He leans backward, a little, to old-fashioned ways of living and feels at home in a house that had nearly a century under its eaves before he entered it. Leaning backward too far, a man can always sit down and think things over. Leaning forward too far, he is likely to fall on his nose.

XXII

I Shall Miss My Debts

On an afternoon in September 1940 a simple ceremony of burial was conducted in our back garden. There were few flowers and no tears. With a lot of innocent merriment, in fact, we laid away in a stone-and-cement sarcophagus the extinct and unlamented second mortgage.

Headstone of the tomb is half a farmyard grindstone, symbolic of what the second mortgage has done to my nose during the past thirteen years. It was a building-and-loan mortgage, which means that I have paid it twice over, dividing the monthly tribute equally between capital and interest. It might have died two years sooner, except that a member of the association ran away some years ago with $160,000. About $2000 of it was mine.

At the burying party the guests were invited to contribute small articles for interment with the mortgage. The idea was borrowed from the Time Capsule at the New York World's Fair of 1939–40, which is supposed to stay buried beneath the swamps of Flushing for the discovery of posterity about five thousand years from now. There is also the Crypt of Civilization, an extracurricular activity of Oglethorpe University, Georgia, which is to be shut tight in 1950 and kept shut until the year 8113, at which time it is to be opened by the State of Georgia, the Government of the United States and "the administration of Oglethorpe University."

The inscription on the still open door admits no doubt that the United States and Oglethorpe University will both be here about six thousand years from now. It seems at this distance that somebody may have done a neat job of publicity for dear old Oglethorpe by building the Crypt of Civilization, but no expense was spared in doing it. The crypt is of impenetrable rock and concrete and the door is a slab of stainless steel.

My Own Four Walls

And to make sure that nobody pokes holes in it until the year 8113, the solemn inscription on the door contains the warning that the crypt's contents include "no jewels or precious stones." If the world should turn honest in the next thousand years, this will stand as a scathing sentence on the morals and manners of the twentieth century.

Our posterity won't have to wait so long, and the inscription on the sarcophagus of the second mortgage is no warning to tomb thieves. It says: "Not to be opened until Christmas 1999."

It turned out to be extraordinarily difficult to select suitable articles for the amusement and admiration of posterity. A great deal of present-day stuff won't keep in a sarcophagus. The ancient Egyptians managed with precious junk of gold and silver, but only the government is permitted to bury gold nowadays. So I settled for a Lincoln penny and a streetcar token.

Somebody else contributed a mousetrap. Mice, he pointed out, may be obsolete by the year 1999. A lady tossed in her lipstick. Somebody else put in an electric-light bulb. The bulb was burned out, but by the year

XXII. I Shall Miss My Debts

1999 it may not matter. By that time the happy home may be illuminated with bottled sunlight.

Possibly I should have included an income-tax report and sweepstakes ticket to show what we did with our money in the year 1940. I did toss in a handful of defunct policies of insurance on the house, furnishings, car and my personal life, of which I have accumulated through the years enough to paper a small bungalow.

One of the ladies present laid away a pair of Nylon stockings, admittedly ruined by runners. Somebody else put in a cigarette and a safety match, wrapped carefully in cellophane. The local tax collector, Hubert Hyatt, one of the honorary pallbearers, contributed a document explaining the nature of a second mortgage for the mystification and astonishment of posterity.

My next-door neighbor dropped in the first tooth lost by her little daughter, Rhona Synnestvedt, in a box neatly tied and labeled. Its original owner may live long enough to reclaim it on Christmas 1999. Edward Davis added to the pile a used safety-razor blade, identified as "one of the outstanding problems of our era." For the same reason somebody wanted to put in a Japanese beetle, but not two beetles. Two beetles, it was pointed out, would probably raise a family and ultimately destroy the sarcophagus and its entire contents.

All present at the ceremony signed their names in indelible ink on a sheet of rag paper. By 1999 many of them will be difficult to identify and most of them will be dead and gone. But the list of their names should be interesting reading.

Not too irreverently, I trust, a mixed chorus of younger members of the family sang something like a hymn, while the tomb was sealed, to the tune of "The Old Oaken Bucket."

> *How near to our hearts was the old second mortgage,*
>   *So tested, so trusted, so tried and so true;*
> *It cost a small fortune in anyone's language,*
>   *Plus numerous charges and interest too.*
> *Farewell to the mortgage on Penepac Manor,*
>   *Where roses are blooming and ivy doth twine;*
> *O first it was Yerkes' and then it was Snyder's,*
>   *And then it was Cranch's, but now it is mine.*

My Own Four Walls

So the tomb was shut and sealed, and over it I turned down an empty glass. Any time I feel like it, hereafter, I can go into the garden and sit on the second mortgage.

I hope this may be remembered in the impending future as a symbolic ceremony. It happened at a time when the Depression which began in 1929, or thereabouts, was showing signs of drying up.

As I stood beside the grave in the twilight I found myself wondering whether I shall miss the second mortgage and the good old Depression when both are gone. Especially the Depression, for we have been together a long time, through thick and thin. Some of it was pretty thick and most of it was pretty thin, but a companionship of many years is not to be lightly tossed aside.

The demise of the mortgage, paid off painfully at the rate of $80 a month, serves to remind me that I have crawled from under a considerable load of debt during the last decade and a half. So have many others who live, labor and have their being in a constant crisis of effort to make a living by working at it. Somehow or other, Depression or no, we have paid off in these years a staggering sum of debt.

When the last boom got dizzy and fell off the band wagon into the slough of despond it was explained by experts that the American people had got out of their depth in debt. The statistics were stupendous. Adding machines broke down in the attempt to total the federal, state, local and municipal debts, plus the personal involvements of people like me in mortgages, installment obligations, back dues at the country club, department-store accounts and all kinds of loans, judgment notes, speculations and margin accounts with stockbrokers.

Some authorities thought that the way out was by borrowing more money, on the general theory that one good debt deserves another. Among them were others, biding their time, who believed in cold blood that repudiation is the best policy.

That is what happened to a lot of big debts but not to many little ones. It is easier to repudiate a monstrous debt than a relatively little one. Annoying little debts are paid; big debts are defaulted. My mortgage, it seems, was destined to be one of the little ones.

Also among those present during the big squeeze were thousands of cheerful bankrupts who got out of debt during the Depression by forgetting

XXII. I Shall Miss My Debts

it. But voluntary bankruptcies are for those who regard the morals of business in no better light than those of contract bridge. Others could not comfortably get off so lightly and proved it in highly practical fashion during the years of the locust by mending their ways of living and paying their debts.

Most of their names are unhonored and unsung. But throughout these lean years a great many middle-income Americans tightened their belts, scaled down their standards of living to the financial facts and steadily reduced their mortgages, obligations, promissory notes and accounts payable as much as possible and reasonable in their straightened circumstances.

It seems to me that they were the forgotten men of our generation. They came through hard times with a minimum of help and sympathy. Nobody ever suggested they should have a bonus, loan or relief ration. Nobody offered to cancel their war debts or protect them against their natural enemies. And before their tribe decreases too much a specimen should be stuffed and mounted in the Smithsonian Institution as a monument to the hard times they suffered and survived. Or he might be cast in imperishable bronze and put on a pedestal in Wall Street for short traders to strike matches on.

But as I ponder the final fate of the mortgage I sometimes wonder what does it profit a man to pay off his debts and be ripe and ready for another trimming when the next depression comes along.

The late Benjamin Franklin preached thrift, though he rarely practiced it, and most moralists maintain that it is a grand, good thing for a man to be out of debt. But I wonder sometimes what might happen to the world, including myself, if all debts were paid.

Nothing much more upsetting could happen to our civilization. For then there would be no more dividends at all, not merely an occasional dud in the safe-deposit box. If debts were paid there would be slim pickings for bankers, who are unable to make money by sitting on it and hatching it. Bankers thrive on debts, and so do their sisters and their cousins and their aunts. When my rural banker lends me money it is assumed he does me a financial favor, but I think I do him one by paying six per cent for it.

In a debtless world, likewise, insurance companies would lose their invisible means of support. Numerous varieties of finance companies,

My Own Four Walls

building societies, brokers, hock shops and installment houses would be left holding an empty bag. There would be no more incomes from mortgages or annuities. If nobody owed any money, no money would be earning a living for the lenders.

This is no merely academic discussion, because I am endeavoring to determine whether it is a good thing that I have whittled away my debts on the grindstone of necessity during the past few years. And whether I should stay out of debt, if I ever get altogether out of it, and possibly become a social menace and economic outlaw by owing nobody any money.

There is evidently something to be said in favor of debts. Not national debts or war debts or bad debts, but the kind of debts which you and I have been worrying about and wearing down during the years of financial famine. Debts like the one whose unmourned corpse lies in my garden sarcophagus.

As the list of them grows less I know that I shall miss them when they are gone.

For experience, to most of us, proves that a decent debt is a steadying and stabilizing influence. Its outstanding example is the reckless extravagance by which an average American gets married, builds and owns a home, raises a family and dies with sufficient insurance to pay the funeral expenses. At the time of life when the normal young man can hardly be trusted with the change from a five-dollar bill he anchors himself to the treadmill with chains of debt. Wife and family, hearth and home, building and loan dues and monthly payments on the electric refrigerator compel him to become a stable citizen and keep him that way.

Signing on the dotted line saves many a man from his naturally vagabond and unsocial instincts. Respectable debts hold him down while he lives so that he may be held down by a respectful tombstone when he dies. He couldn't own his own home without borrowing to buy or build it. Sometimes he buys his babies on the installment plan, as well as the parlor furniture. And his debts drive him on to bigger and better things, which often means to bigger and better debts and obligations.

It may be that the real foundations of middle and lower class society in the United States are the first and second mortgages. These regulate the birth rate, control standards of living, create suburban communities

XXII. I Shall Miss My Debts

and account for the existence of contract bridge, chain stores and nine tenths of the women's clubs and golf courses.

I suspect, too, that ambition owes something to borrowing ability, whether money be borrowed outright or the same result is achieved by stretching credit with the butcher, baker and department store. And how many men, I wonder, have hauled themselves to the heights of success by their own shoe straps, mainly by trying to get out of the mire of debt? How many have financed fame and fortune on credit? How many have won a sound credit rating by borrowing and repaying, by running up bills and meeting them?

These considerations may sufficiently account for my concern over my vanishing debts. But we may further consider what might happen if an economic miracle should wipe them out altogether. Let us suppose that some benevolent relative should die suddenly and leave me $20,000. We may as well make it $50,000, since this is only a game. It couldn't really happen, because my close relatives are either too poor or too close to leave me anything. Perhaps it would be more plausible to imagine that the Federal Government has given me $50,000, having exhausted all other ways and means of unbalancing the budget.

The immediate result would be that I would develop my latent talent for putting off till tomorrow what I don't want to do today. Like every optimistic owner of a sweepstakes ticket, I am resolved that sudden wealth shall never teach me bad habits, but that is because I have never tried it.

More likely I should learn very quickly to make nine minutes' worth of mail last all morning and a lunch-table conference wreck the whole afternoon and leave me fit for nothing but eighteen holes of golf. As a writer, I would highly resolve to write an enduring novel but would never be in the mood for it until a week from Wednesday.

My health would suffer a similar disintegration. A distressing effect of owning $50,000 is the need for three annual vacations and two dozen long week ends. These would pave the way for several unnecessary operations for which, at present, I can afford neither time nor money.

I would also set seriously about the business of ruining my children, partly by allowing them all the debilitating luxuries which their little hearts desire. This might exhaust the $50,000 rather rapidly, and by the time it was gone I would have lost something much more important than $50,000.

My Own Four Walls

You don't suppose it would work out that way if $50,000 fell in your lap some fine morning. But if you cannot make $50,000, what makes you think you could manage that much money? In my own case I am convinced that if dumb luck should bring me $50,000 dumber luck would soon lose it.

There is no momentary danger of my demoralization by an overdose of easy money. There is yet another mortgage leering at my remaining money-making abilities. But something warns me, even now, that when the last debt is paid the work horse will miss his spurs. There will be less point in making money, more excuses for spending it.

So I shall miss my debts if I ever succeed in paying them. Miss them so badly that it may be well and wise to be looking about for new ones. Debts not so wide as a barn door, nor deep as a well, but big enough to keep me out of mischief while I work at them and worry about them. And in this philosophy, perhaps, there are some political implications.

What this country needs, maybe, is bigger and better borrowing by the people, from the people and for the people, and much less borrowing by the government, from the people, for the benefit of anybody who can prove that he is unlikely to repay the loan and hardly capable of doing so.

It seems to me that a man sits on top of the world when he has sufficient spending money for his reasonable needs, a little leeway of credit in emergency or moments of opportunity and a bearable burden of debts payable. A nation is sitting pretty under the same three conditions, but not otherwise. And there was never a good stool with less than three sound legs. Credit is good, cash in hand is better, but the balance wheel of progress is debt.

So I shall miss my debts when they are gone. A lot of other people will miss them. They have done their small share to steady the ship through the rough waters of depression, and their smallest payments on account have been gratefully received. Some have practically served as ten-year endowment policies to my creditors.

Vast industries are earnestly anxious that I should get into debt again, as deep and soon as possible. So are a variety of salesmen, bankers, brokers, accountants, contractors and real-estate operators. But I am not worrying about my debt dependents. I am worrying because I shall hardly be

XXII. I Shall Miss My Debts

able to face a future in which the first of the month is merely a date on the calendar.

These debts of mine, including the second mortgage, have kept me company in good times and bad, in sickness and health, for better or worse. They have kept me out of mischief, perhaps out of jail. I would be lost and strayed in a strange and dangerous world without them. For prosperity has its perils, as well as adversity, and perhaps an uncomfortable frying pan is better than a consuming fire.

XXIII

Est Mihi Rus Minimum

A quotation out of its context is likely to pick up meanings which its original author never intended. Will Shakespeare, very likely, would be much astonished to hear modern Americans misquoting "I knew him, Horatio." It was not a very vital point in *Hamlet* that the Prince of Denmark knew poor Yorick, and Shakespeare dismisses it with few words.

It might surprise Diogenes, too, who went looking for a man, to find the modern world insisting that he must be an honest man. All Diogenes wanted was a man.

Most quotations must be mistrusted. I speak by experience, for in an imaginary conversation with Shakespeare I once wrote the phrase, "He who keeps a garden hath a daily beauty in his life." Readers like it and wanted to know in which play Shakespeare said it. Shakespeare didn't say it. I said it. And when it is credited to Shakespeare in somebody's new book of quotations I shall deserve the blame for it.

More serious is the change of meaning which may come upon a sentence when it stands in splendid isolation. Engraved in cement around the chimney of my outdoor fireplace is a line from the Roman poet and epigrammatist, Martial. "Est mihi rus minimum. Sitque precor longum." It is an excellent conversation piece for garden picnics and cocktail parties, because nobody remembers enough Latin to interpret it. So I must translate it, which is something to talk about when company calls.

"I have a little home in the country," said Martial, "and I pray I may have it a long time." It sounds like the preface to a poem in praise of country life or a tribute to the old homestead. Horace and Ovid went in for that sort of thing, writing of farms and vineyards and bucolic employments while living in comfortably steam-heated Roman apartments. So why not Martial?

XXIII. Est Mihi Rus Minimum

Having set the inscription firmly and forever in the stonework of the fireplace, I turned to Martial to read the rest of it.

Martial was not writing in favor of the simple and rural life. He was complaining bitterly to Caesar because he wasn't connected with the local waterworks. Most of the neighbors had running water in their homes, but his "rus minimum" was dry. It made matters worse that Martial could hear the water running in the Marcian aqueduct, just around the corner. So he tossed off a dozen lines of Latin verse in hopes that Augustus would take pity on his plight and send a plumber.

Those who yearn for a little home in the country should bear in mind the plumbing problem. There are also the problems of light and heat, telephone and rapid transit. The simple life of our forefathers looks its best at a safe distance. On close acquaintance bucolic peace, quiet and inconvenience can be a bore and hardship.

I marvel at the privations endured by those who built and inhabited my four walls before I bought them and built a new house inside them and a new garden outside. They pumped their water from an eighteen-foot well. They stored milk and butter in a springhouse a hundred yards

My Own Four Walls

from the kitchen door. They heated the living room with a round-bellied stove, an ingenious device for broiling you on one side and freezing you on the other. They lightened their evenings with kerosene lamps and candles.

Twenty-two years and tremendous expenditures have remedied most of these deficiencies. But I like to believe that this is still a "rus minimum," though so changed that its own grandmother might disown it. It is still a little home in the country, though not so little as it used to be. The country, also, is less than it used to be, but the view from all our windows is still thick with trees and the clatter of modern traffic passes by a quarter mile away. Birds and squirrels are our neighbors and the stars of a summer night shine undimmed by city lights and dust.

It is a country home, too, in the respect that I live forty-five minutes from my day's work in Philadelphia, about as far away, in traveling time, as those sections of the city that must be reached by subway and a streetcar transfer. City dwellers envy my rural retreat in summertime and sympathize with my isolation in winter. It does not occur to them that I can reach my doorstep as quickly as they can, though not so cheaply.

But the charm of a country home, be it ever so humble, is not altogether its aloofness from the city's stress and roar and striving. It lies no less in the fact that its owner may do with it as he will, without fear of zoning laws and building inspectors. In the country a man's home may still be his castle. Not even the neighbors may quarrel with his alterations and repairs. No necessity commands him to match his home with the house next door or grow the same stuff in his garden.

So a man may leave his mark on a little land and a little home in the country. He may have greater pride in their possession than any city dweller in his. He may understand what Thomas Carlyle was thinking and feeling when he wrote:

> *My whinstone house my castle is;*
> *These are my own four walls.*

I have been unable to find out what specific house Carlyle was writing about. These two lines are quoted in many books as derived from a poem called *My Own Four Walls*, but literary authorities and expert librarians have been unable to locate the rest of it. And when a librarian

XXIII. Est Mihi Rus Minimum

can't track a line of poetry to its original lair she is a miserably unhappy creature.

A whinstone house, anyway, is one built of local stone, usually scrap stone, rather than quarried, which would be called field stone in this country. Mine is a whinstone house. This is my castle, these are my own four walls.

It is not quite reasonable that I should think of them as altogether my own. Owners of the first mortgage have something to say on that point, and the records show that I have had it only twenty-two years and others more than a century.

But I recall a pleasant book by Hulbert Footner, called *Charles' Gift*, which is the name of his home in South Maryland, a house "as comfortable to put on as an old suit of clothes" and perhaps the oldest in the state. It tells how Mr Footner feels about his house. He has lived there only about thirty years but is beginning to believe that he was born there in 1650 or that he built the place himself.

If he has had the same kind of fun and troubles with an old house that I have, he did build most of it. After a few determined years of alterations and amendments there is likely to be little left of an old house except two thirds of the walls, the chimneys and the foundations. The rest has been replaced, stick by stick and stone by stone, in a continual campaign to keep the house and family from subsiding into the cellar.

But it must be noted that Mr Footner was able to write a book about his house, though he did not build it, as I have written one about mine. Nobody could write a book about a six-room apartment or a hotel room. A house is different, especially a house where many generations have lived and left their fingerprints.

An old house has personality and character, sometimes stronger than those of its inhabitants. History hangs around old houses and vanishes into thin air when they disappear. That is why I have sometimes wished that George Washington might have slept one night, at least, in our old farmhouse. It is something of a wonder that he didn't, since he seems to have spent most of the Revolutionary War sleeping in the old inns and farmhouses of Montgomery County. One reason why he didn't, perhaps, is that the house wasn't here when George Washington was fighting and losing the battle Germantown. Otherwise my home's history might be a more significant tale.

My Own Four Walls

I see eye to eye with Mr Footner when he rejoices that his youngsters are growing up to regard Charles' Gift as the old homestead. It doesn't matter to them that the house was there two centuries before they were. My own infants, now beginning to scatter themselves abroad, feel the same way about our moss-covered and moth-eaten mansion. Some of them may yet be bragging that they were born there, as were nine of them. I think they should, because it is a good thing to be born somewhere. It is very sad that millions of Americans in the world of tomorrow will have to admit that their only birthplace was the fourteenth floor of a city hospital. Even presidents and postmasters general will have no birthplace to call their own. But people without birthplaces might almost as well be cases of spontaneous combustion, which is one argument in favor of an old house and being born within its walls.

I like my own four walls no less that Mr Footner cares for his. My house gives me sympathy for the past and hope for the future. It reflects the inspiring industry of its previous inhabitants plus my own feeble contributions. It fits my asymmetric personality comfortably, like my working trousers. They also have a history, personality and atmosphere. I bought them on a trip to England some years ago, and the stubborn genius of the Anglo-Saxon race is built into their fabric and structure. They are not beautiful, but time, decay and the old-clothesman cast envious eyes on them in vain. They will never wear out, though they may be patched, and I expect someday to be buried in them.

So it may be with a house, but the house must be worth keeping and mending and enlarging to meet the expanding needs of its occupants. Mine was made that way a long while ago. Several generations of jerry-building have come and gone since then. More will pass before my four walls fall down.

There are signs and portents that a lot of Americans are now looking around for some place where they may get roots into the soil. Restlessness is not really our national nature. There were pioneering and wandering in the brave days of old, but their purpose was to find a place for long settlement. And many Americans again are yearning for houses and a little land, not yearly leases and arguments with janitors and building superintendents. Many must build their own or go without, but some choose wisely when they take an old and seasoned house and make it over for modern living.

XXIII. Est Mihi Rus Minimum

Visitors sometimes wonder why I don't own a nice new house with tiled bathrooms and built-in breakfast nooks and a set of chimes to give warning when somebody comes to the front door to sell magazine subscriptions. It is difficult to explain that I don't want one. It is hard to convince them that a ready-made home becomes a rigid frame around family life, imposing its pattern on those who live within its walls. I try to tell them, too, that I don't want a new house because I shall not be permitted to have a hand in building it nor allowed to change it from year to year. Another good reason is that I can't afford one.

There is a scrap of verse which haunts my memory from childhood days.

> *Leaned on his gate he gazes; tears*
> *Are in his eyes, and in his ears*
> *The murmur of a thousand years.*

I am not quite clear what the poet is talking about, which probably indicates that this is good poetry. But a man leaning on his own gate makes a pleasant picture. I should like to lean on my own gate, if I had a gate, and I shall consider sometime where to put a gate for leaning and gazing purposes.

There is no need for tears, but a man should be able to lean on his own gate and gaze at the work of his hands. He should be allowed to gaze back through the years at the changes time and hard labor have wrought. It is pleasant, even without leaning on a gate, to remember the wreck and ruin of this old farmhouse in 1918, its broken picket fences, its faded yellow plaster, its disreputable porch and dispirited garden. It is pleasant to sit on the tomb of the second mortgage and smoke the pipe of peace in the twilight, meditating on what has gone before and wondering what next.

"And in his ears the murmur of a thousand years." Not a thousand, but more than a century since this house was raised from the rocks of its own soil and the sand of its own cellar. Then these tall trees were seedlings, the children of Penn's Woods. Then Philadelphia was half a day's journey away, but mill wheels turned in the valley and there was a living in the land. Now we live on the land and labor somewhere else, except that I am permitted, by courtesy of an old American house and encouragement of

My Own Four Walls

those who lived there before I was born in England, to turn my hand for the fun of it to the trades and skills of long ago.

On a summer evening the sun lingers in a hollow of the hills and fingers of light thread through the willow tree to lay a golden pattern on the lawn. The house looms dark against the twilight, its ancient shape not too much spoiled by my meddling. The bullfrog burps reflectively in the lily pool. The feet of my friendly ghosts rustle beneath the twisted apple trees they planted. There is no gate to lean upon, but I can lay aside my long-handled shovel and sit on the ivied wall where once the smokehouse stood. Flowers are in friendly bloom, and the corn and beans are prospering.

"Est mihi rus minimum. Sitque precor longum." These are my own four walls.

Index

Asplundh, Oswald 144–145
Aswell, Edward C. 82

The Battlements 125–126
Bostock, Ed 20–21
Branin, Newt 18, 96–97
Bryn Athyn, Pa. 1, 15, 50–54, 56, 59, 64, 67
Bryn Athyn Cathedral 32, 51–52, 117

Childs, Randolph 100
Cooper, Fred 96
Cooper, Will 54
Crypt of Civilization, Oglethorpe University 159

Davis, Edward 161

Ellis Island 2, 13–14

Finkeldey, Fred 15, 92

Grakelow, Charles 70

Heaton, George 70
House, Jay 3–4, 129
Howard, Leslie 4, 125–126
Hyatt, Hubert 161
Hyatt, Winfred 144

Johnson, Herbert 16

Keach, Elias 43
Kendrick, Freeland 70
Kintner, Charlie 147

Larue, Lafe 65
Laurence, Earl of Ferrers 10
Leary's Book Store 76, 78–79

Montague, Dr. J.F. 82–83
Morrison, Charles 149

Odhner, Loyal 68, 92

Paddleford, Clementine 140
Penn, William 43, 45
Pitcairn, John 50
Public Ledger newspaper 3–5, 76, 109, 149

Rose family coat of arms 10
Rosenquist, Victor 117

St. Paul (ship) 12
Swedenborg, Emanuel 1–2, 50–53
Swedenborgians 1–2, 50–53
Synnestvedt, Kenneth 46
Synnestvedt, Rhona 161

Townsend, Frank 82

Van Horn, John Frederick 64–67

Webster, John 23, 25, 28–29, 32, 36, 44, 62, 75
Wells, Col. John A. 55–56
Wells, Marjorie 2
Whitehead, William 50

Yerkes, Ben 22–31, 38, 43–44, 53–54, 56, 61–62, 90, 125, 142, 148–149, 161